Hedgehopping Aviation

A Book for Pilots by a Pilot

Clyde E. Roach

authorHOUSE®

AuthorHouse™
1663 Liberty Drive
Bloomington, IN 47403
www.authorhouse.com
Phone: 1-800-839-8640

First published by AuthorHouse 7/2/2009

ISBN: 978-1-4389-6137-8 (e)
ISBN: 978-1-4389-6135-4 (sc)
ISBN: 978-1-4389-6136-1 (hc)

Library of Congress Control Number: 2009904860

Printed in the United States of America
Bloomington, Indiana

This book is printed on acid-free paper.

Contents

PROLOGUE

I write this book as an old man with the aim of passing on information that may be of benefit to pilots, would be pilots, or any other inquiring persons. If we don't pass on information from one generation to the next, we are doomed. We sent a man to the moon using information gained from previous generations. Suppose each generation had to reinvent the wheel. You never know when unrelated information will become related.

A supposition among some doctors expresses the belief: sight is learned the first year of life. If a baby is blindfolded at birth, and could not see for the first year, the baby would be blind for life. Reason: it's too late to learn to see. This may be true, to a point. Nevertheless, you are never too young or too old to learn. Just this year I learned enriched uranium is not radioactive. You might ask, What does that have to do with piloting? It is the learning process that matters. Memory is even more important.

Airplane accidents and incidents that I have in some way been involved, will be highlighted along with some stories. Sometimes we are our own worst enemy. All accidents and incidents are caused by human failure of some kind – from which, we can learn.

When placing blame for aircraft accidents, many origins are considered. Designers, manufacturers, and people who make the rules have a responsibility. Nevertheless, pilots will always be first choice.

From my mistakes and successes, you might learn something. If not, you may enjoy the stories. All statements about aircraft and aircraft systems are derived from hands on experience. Bear in mind; I have no formal education in the realm engineering or aeronautics. I will log all the information I can remember and hope it will be of benefit to veterans as well as beginners.

I am an 88-year-old retired airline pilot with considerable hands on experience in safety, training and engineering. My aviation background encompasses time spent with Eastern Airlines as cleaner, mechanic's helper, and commissary clerk. When World War Two came along, I joined the US Army Air Corps and learned to fly. During World War Two, I saw service in the European and Africa theater, dropping paratroopers, pulling gliders, and flying resupply missions. I was shot down only once. Flying time exceeds 25,000 hours. Forty years with Eastern Airlines included duty as copilot, test pilot, line captain, check captain, flight instructor, FAA designee, ALPA safety representative, and fuel specialist. After retirement, I did some work as an aeronautical consultant.

Safety of commercial aviation continues to improve. The Airline Pilots Association has been the driving force contributing to progress. The FAA is charged, by law, to oversee safety and promote civil aviation. This is like sending the fox to guard the henhouse. This dual purpose makes it impossible to do a good job in both endeavors. Airlines are in business to make money. Safety is expensive. Lives are irreplaceable. Therefore, pilots will continue to be the driving force for improved safety. If you don't do your part, all will suffer.

Anyone can learn to fly, as you will see by example.

This work is unedited. Find any errors, blame me.

Clyde E. Roach

CHAPTER ONE
FUEL

Cliche: The only time you have too much fuel is when you are on fire. Nevertheless, there is more to it than that. Exploring minds sometimes ask, why is there a minimum and maximum temperature limitation for in-flight. Some people think, the colder the better. Temperature limitation for the DC-8 in-flight was -79 degrees C to standard +35 degrees C. The colder limitation is to protect fuel from congealing. Fuel may begin to congeal before reaching the limitation.

In early jet operation concern was real. Engines have a fuel heater, but this only heats fuel entering the fuel control unit. Fuel in the tanks will congeal if temperature is low enough. Experts advised us, if this occurs, the only recourse is to increase speed and hope friction will raise the temperature, or find warmer temperature. This might be an easy task with no engines operating.

The only incident of this nature, in my memory, occurred near the equator. Due to the egg shape of the troposphere, it may extend to 35,000 feet at the equator. At the poles, it may end as low as 8,000 feet. The coldest atmosphere at high altitudes is near the equator. Less you forget; a standard lapse rate occurs only to the top of the troposphere. I wouldn't worry about fuel congealing. Too many other more important hurdles exist.

FAA flight inspectors were required once a year to complete a recurrent training program that consisted of a simulator period and a check ride in the airplane. Eastern provided the training on a contract basis.

I was giving an oral examination to two FAA inspectors before the check ride. The first question was, "What kinds of fuel do we use." One answered kerosene and the other answered, " JP4". Both were wrong. The next question was, "What color is the fuel?" Neither knew. I informed them, "When I first learned to fly an airplane, we thought it important to get plenty of fuel, and the right kind. When fluid is observed leaking out of an airplane, it's good to be able to identify it." I tried not to hurt their feelings. Some FAA inspectors were denied employment with airlines. Employment with FAA was second choice. You should not forget the elementary stuff. When taking an oral, be prepared for anything.

On a DC8/63 charter flight from Miami to Caracas, Venezuela; after landing, before I got out of the airplane, the fueling crew was pumping fuel into the tanks from on top of the wing. Normal fueling is accomplished from under wing. On the way in I had run one tank dry. Fueling a tank from over the wing is prohibited, if the tank is empty. This I knew. It had been in Federal Air Regulations for many years. I had no idea why. Returning to Miami, as OAT (Operation and Training) Chairman, my next project was to research the 'why'.

This is what I discovered. The British were the first to fly a commercial jet, the "Comet". The first one was lost to an in flight explosion. The investigation centered around a possible fuel explosion. The cause of this accident was later determined to be a <u>pressurization blow out</u> and not a fuel explosion. Much was learned about the inherent jet fuel characteristic of self ignition.

A chamber to house a Comet fuel cell was built. Pressure and temperature inside the tank was controlled. Arrangements were made to shake or vibrate the fuel cell. When the temperature reached the flash point (temperature at which fuel will ignite if an ignition point is introduced), and while shaking, the whole thing blew up.

When fuel is agitated from shaking, splashing, or being pumped through a pipe, it generates static electricity just as you do when walking across a rug, stick a key in a door lock, and a spark is discharged. The flash point of fuel changes a little with pressure altitude, and with oxygen content of the vapor above the fuel. Oxygen is added to the vapor when fuel is agitated. Making it more volatile.

In a landing accident in Italy, an airplane slid down the runway shedding its engines, which came to rest as the fuselage continued to slide. The ruptured fuel tanks left a stream of fuel leading from the engines to the fuselage. A fire started at the engines, and progressed toward the fuselage. The slow burning kerosene allowed time for all the passengers to escape. Had the fuel been type A (in use today), the passengers would have burned to death.

Standard fuel for jets in the beginning was kerosene. When we were using slow burning kerosene for fuel, no probation existed against in-flight dumping fuel with an on-board or engine fire. No minium speed regulation existed. The burning rate of kerosene is so slow, even though the fuel might be ignited, the flame would be blown away from the aircraft at any speed. This does not apply to any JP. After ten years operating with JP, our manuals did not reflect this informational change.

Early jet engines dumped a small amount of fuel on every takeoff. When jet engines are shut down, a small amount of unburned fuel remains in the engine. To keep this fuel from draining to the ground, it was directed to a small holding tank. On each subsequent takeoff, the fuel was dumped overboard, creating pollution – no fish in nearby lakes. If you want to get rid of mosquitoes, dump a little kerosene on the water. This will also destroy the aquatic food chain. Due to environmental pressure, a system was developed to return the residual fuel to a main tank.

Before jets, about the only use for kerosene was for lamps and heating. The demand was low and the price only half that of gasoline. By the mid 1960's, Eastern Airlines in Miami was pumping more jet fuel (JP) than all the gasoline pumped by all the service stations in Dade County combined. The crude oil refining process produces only a small percentage of kerosene. With increased demand, prices rose and availability decreased. There is a limited amount of kerosene that can be refined from crude oil, and it is needed for production of jet fuel.

Jet fuel in use by airlines when I retired was known as Type A -- JP1, JP4, JP5 , or any mixture thereof. All have different specific gravities and flash points. This means, if your fuel totalizer is not calibrated for the fuel on board, the reading will not be completely accurate. One of our DC-8s filled all tanks with kerosene. Since kerosene is heavier, Douglas claimed the wing had been over stressed. JP is kerosene based with various amounts of gasoline type additives. When any amount of gasoline is added to kerosene, it becomes highly explosive. JP4, with the lowest flash point, is the lightest and most explosive and gives more power. JP5, the heaviest, has the highest flash point, and produces more BTUs, thus more range. The difference is slight. At one time, armed services used JP-4 in fighters and JP5 in transports. There are other JP numbers that are inconsequential to airline operation.

Much of this information came from Director Fuel NASA. Gasoline has the lowest flash point, and is therefore more dangerous. Many fires and explosions have occurred at gasoline stations. The most common cause has been fueling a portable container sitting in the back of a pickup truck. Older truck manuals reflected this danger with a blurb suggesting the container be placed on the ground before fueling. During the depression of the 1930s, we mixed cheaper kerosene with gasoline used in model T Fords. It worked fine, and saved money.

To prevent self-ignition when fueling airplanes, Federal Regulations have always prohibited over-wing fueling if the tank is empty, or in flight transfer of fuel from one tank to another (to prevent splashing, which generates static electricity). Over wing fueling is permitted only if the tank has enough fuel in it to allow submersion of the nozzle before pumping, and many other precautions are taken. If an airliner sat on the ground with all tanks empty and no way to use the under-wing fueling system, the airplane would have to be junked. Or maybe the FAA would make another rule. JP4 is now banned by some airlines.

Pan American fuellers in San Juan added fuel to an Electra for another carrier. One tank was empty, and they chose to fill from over wing. The resulting fire did great damage. There have been many fires and explosions related to fueling for various reasons. Air Force regulations prohibit ground fueling if a thunderstorm is within ten miles. Commercial regulations are not as stringent.

Commercial regulations do not apply to the Air Force. In the beginning of in-flight refueling, many Air Force tankers were lost due to static generated explosions. Now military tanks are nitrogen charged or other systems exist to prevent explosions. Not so with commercial jets, because of the expense. The SST uses transfer of fuel in flight for ballast, but an antistatic additive is required for dispatch.

In the early days of JP usage a Pan American Boeing exploded in-flight near Baltimore. The NTSB declared a lightning strike as the probable cause. Evidence was present that the tip tank exploded. No evidence of a lightning strike materialize. The flight was experiencing turbulence, and I think the fuel may have exploded due to self ignition through agitation. Tip tanks contained no baffles to prevent slouching, and were connected to a main tank only by drainage (no pumps). No one has ever measured fuel temperature after the airplane has been subjected sunlight or temperature rise from high speed cruise at low altitude. Someone must have agreed with me, because immediately after the accident, baffles were installed in all tip tanks, to prevent slouching. The B-727, built later, has so many baffles in the tanks to prevent sloshing, if you open all valves, it takes many hours for the fuel to seep from one tank to another.

The fuel dumping system on all of our B-720s was modified, which required a flight test. Tanks to be tested were supposed to be filled with water. On test flights, to save time, we made the dump just after takeoff over populated areas, sometimes below 100 feet. Maintenance screwed up, fuel, not water, was in all tanks to be tested. Dumping fuel at low speed is dangerous, but can be done. I often wondered if people on the ground smelled JP.

In the early years without radar or good weather forecasting, we were subjected to long flights in instrument conditions. To determine when static electricity was building on the airplane, the high frequency radio was always in our ear. Static buildup blocked reception, and generated a scratchy interference. A change of airspeed would sometimes extinguish the interference, and possibly avoid a lightening strike. Static was also an indication of rough air ahead. The strike can come from either direction, to or from the aircraft. All airplanes in flight generate static electricity. The charge may be + or -. Atmosphere is also charged + or -. All you need for a strike is sufficient polarity. Lightening strikes airliners on average once a day with no ill effect. Static arresters are a no-go item. I doubt if you have HF radios anymore.

After digesting all this information, I had a telephone conversation with Eastern Airlines President Frank Borman on the subject. He was so unconcerned and uncooperative that I immediately reported EAL to the FAA for violation of fueling regulations. The result of which was a host of revised fueling regulations, which were totally unsatisfactory, and had to be revised again, and again. I was astounded by the lack of knowledge coming from experts. Learn all you can. Don't depend entirely on experts.

I asked the company for our fuel specifications and was advised, "All Eastern fuel has an antistatic additive." Specifications received from our major supplier proved this to be a blatant lie. EAL never used any antistatic additive.

It has been many years since the TWA 800 accident. The NTSB announced that the center fuel tank of the Boeing 747 exploded, but they have been unable to identify the ignition source. It seems quite logical that the ignition point may have been produced through agitation.

It is known that the center fuel tank was empty (residual fuel, enough for one hell of an explosion). On an NTSB test flight to duplicate the ill-fated one, fuel temperature in the center tank was found to be at the flash point. The CVR (cockpit voice recorder) revealed a fuel imbalance problem, and the fuel pump in that tank was conceivably on. This would have created enough static electricity, through splashing, for an ignition point. Static arresters in the fuel system may not have been installed in the right places – none in the tanks.

Another possibility, since there was a fuel balance problem, the center fuel tank selector valve could have been open. Electric or manual valves have been known to fail. In which case, fuel was being transferred into an empty tank would cause much agitation and splashing. If neither of these suppositions were true, a faulty check valve between the fueling manifold and tank could have caused massive fuel turbulence. The fueling manifold is always pressurized.

This was not the first in-flight explosion, and I am afraid it will not be the last. This was the third unexplained B-747 to explode in flight. Other in-flight explosions also remain unsolved.

After the accident, the NTSB conducted exhaustive tests to pinpoint the source of ignition. All efforts failed. The NTSB declared, "Static electricity that might have been present would not have been enough to ignite the vapors." Although, tests by independent laboratories repeatedly ignited the vapors, under the same conditions, with a spark of only one mill-joule. A joule is a measurement of energy – electricity. One mill-joule is one-one thousands of a joule. The spark generated when you walk across a rug, and touch a key to a lock, is of a magnitude of a minimum of one whole joule. A thousand times more powerful than a mill-joule. The ignition system of a jet engine produces from four to seven joules. This information should have been enough to ring a bell.

Had self ignition of fuel been declared the cause of this accident, public demand would have required immediate steps to prevent the recurrence. Costs would have been enormous.

CHAPTER TWO
GANDER ACCIDENT

Arrow DC-8/63

On December 12, 1985, at about 6:45 A.M. local time, an Arrow Air DC-8/63, with 248 passengers and a crew of eight began its takeoff down Runway 22 at Gander, Newfoundland. The passengers, all (all but eleven) were members of the US Army 101st. Airborne Division, who were being returned home from military observer duties in the Middle East. Within two or three seconds of lift off, it became evident that something was terribly wrong. After a short climb, the aircraft began to lose speed, stalled and, while turning slightly right, struck down-sloping terrain near the top of a wooded hillside, 2975 feet beyond the departure end of the runway, a distance of 720 feet to the right of the extended runway center line. All 256 occupants perished in this tragic accident, the most serious in Canadian aviation history.

The Canadian Aviation Safety Board (CASB) was notified immediately, and within hours the first members of what would become a large team of investigators were on their way to Gander. This began one of the most complex, difficult, and lengthy investigation ever undertaken by the CASB or its predecessor, the Aviation Safety Bureau.

The crash and ensuing fire destroyed the aircraft. There were few witnesses and most had little more than a glimpse of the aircraft during takeoff. The flight data recorder (FDR) was recovered, but it was an old foil-type in poor condition. It contained limited information. The cockpit voice recorder (CVR) was also recovered. It was in generally good condition, but when played back, it was found that the cockpit area microphone channel had not been working. Conversations and ambient sounds were not recorded. Although control tower tapes were available, limited evidence was available to investigators for piecing together the sequence of events that resulted in the accident.

The CASB obtained testimony from various sources which included representatives from the NTSB, Arrow Air, the US Army, the aircraft manufacturer (Mc Donnell Douglas), the engine manufacturer, (Pratt & Whitney), and the FAA. Using the standard International Civil Aviation Organization (ICAO) accident investigation system, they began their work. This system is based on the scientific method; facts are gathered, organized into a logical sequence, analyzed and then they formulate conclusions.

Arrangements were made between the Provincial Government of Newfoundland, the US Army, and the CASB to have the bodies of the victims transported to Dover, Delaware for positive identification and autopsy. Where possible, toxicological samples were taken and sent to the National health & Welfare Lab at Downsview, Ontario. Items of wreckage which investigators thought might help explain the cause of the crash, such as aircraft instruments, engines, thrust reversers and control actuators were shipped to the CASB Safety Laboratory at Uplands for detailed examination and analysis.

The CASB conducted a seven-day public inquiry into this accident beginning on April 8, 1986 in Hull, Quebec. Participants in the inquiry, besides those named above, were the flight crew next-of-kin, the Canadian Department of Transport, the Department of Justice, and the Province of Newfoundland. In all, 43 witnesses testified. Most all the witness, for variable reasons, had an interest in the probable cause that would be rendered. Everyone tried to point the blame away from those they represented. If they could prove that anyone was at fault, liability would be tremendous.

After all of this you might think some definitive conclusions would be forthcoming, but that was not so. CASB members disagreed on the probable cause. Five thought ice on the leading edge of the wings was the cause. Four thought the cause to be a bomb or an in-flight fire. There was absolutely no evidence of either. Until this time, the CASB had a worldwide impeccable reputation for accident investigation. Some of their assumptions were ridiculous. If the amount of ice claimed to be on the wings could have caused the crash, there would be pieces of DC-8s strewn over fields adjacent to most airports in the country.

They should have discredited the theory of ice with testimony of weather conditions, and the fact that an experienced flight engineer was seen looking at the wings on a well- lighted ramp during the pre-flight inspection. Also, the fueling crew agreed, there was no ice. Fuellers work with the deicing crew and are instructed to check for ice. When fueling, their face is very close to the leading edge of the wing.

The bomb and fire theory were beat to death, but no substantiating evidence appeared. The Canadian armed forces made a shoulder to shoulder search of the airport and the ground beneath the trajectory of the flight. They found nothing. Suspect pieces of the wreckage were sent to laboratories for scrutiny. A covering roof was built over the crash site to protect it from weather. It must have covered two or three acres. The soil was examined to a depth of 18 inches, and no evidence of a bomb blast was found.

After recovering the bodies, officials came up with the number 255. One was missing. Repeated searches found the missing body under the roots of a tree that was standing upright. The airplane had knocked over the tree, and a body was deposited in the cavity vacated by the roots. After the plane passed, the tree sprang back to the upright position.

The fire theory was based on autopsy evidence that a chemical was found in the lungs of four or five victims that could have come only from breathing smoke. These victims had sustained injuries that produced instant death in the crash. Thus, could not have breathed the smoke after the explosion. Thus the supposition -- they breathed the smoke before the crash. The lungs of cigarette smokers always contain this chemical, but these four or five were not smokers. How did the investigators know they were non smokers? They asked the parents. These were a bunch of 19 and 20-year-old boys. How many young men smoke and their parents are not aware? I estimated at least 60% of the passengers were smokers.

What about secondhand smoke? I once flew a regular passenger flight on a DC-8 which was instrumented to determine air replacement. Results revealed almost no exchange of air in the rear section of the cabin. Regulations require enough air be pumped into the cabin to exchange all air every three minutes. Certification tests may be true, but not in the rear cabin. Aircraft manufacturers are not flawless, nor are the people who certify.

The Canadian Parliament, after the final accident report was released, lost confidence in the CASB, and completely disbanded it. A former Supreme Court Justice, Willard Eatey, was appointed to review and investigate the entire record of the Gander crash. He issued a report that explained nothing.

I believe the CASB's failure was caused by a lack of knowledge of what the DC-8 will, and will not, do. They were forced to rely on information received from manufacturers, whose primary concern was the time-honored PYA (protect your ass). Computer produced information was used. Manufacturers controlled that too.

My extensive and varied experience flying the DC-8 gave me a definite advantage in putting the pieces together. Eastern Airlines once owned the airplane that crashed, #950. I had flown it often.

Carl Hoffman, a pilot and one hell of an attorney, flew second officer for me on the B-727. He practiced law while flying for EAL. Sitting at the engineer's panel, reading legal briefs, he could still do the job. Years later, flying captain, his law practice was getting so large, early retirement was his choice. Carl represented the survivors of the second officer in a wrongful death law suit. The law firm of Barranco, Kellough, and Kircher represented survivors of the first officer. Legal claims by soldiers survivors were settled by the US government. International law limits recovery to $75,000 in wrongful death civil suits in accidents occurring outside the US, unless intentional or willful negligence can be proven. Lawyers don't like this type case unless they are on solid ground.

My tennis partner, Frank Harrell, a retired FAA inspector who had been acting as a consultant on the case, got me interested. He kept asking me questions about the DC-8 systems, and I finally told him, "Tell those lawyers if they want information to hire me." Both legal firms hired me.

To prepare for the case; I read all the testimony of all the witnesses' appearing at the CASB hearings, all laboratory reports, all committee reports, autopsy and toxicological reports, and many depositions relating to the accident. On one trip down town to Kellough's office, he gave so much to read, I couldn't carry it all and had to make two trips. I also studied the flight data and cockpit voice recorder readouts.

Carl, another attorney from Atlanta, a retired NTSB investigator, and I, flew to Gander. There we flew the takeoff trajectory in a light twin engine aircraft, three times. This gave us a more clear vision of what was going on in the cockpit. We also toured the crash site on foot and talked with some eyewitnesses. At night we stood on the perimeter road and watched the planes takeoff to observe engine exhaust and reflected light. With Jack Lipscomb, a retired NTSB engine investigator, I inspected the wreckage in Ottawa, Canada, where it had been stored.

In Ottawa the investigators did a magnificent job in constructing a small scale topographical model duplicating the path of the airplane at the crash site. As the airplane descended into the trees, it cut a swath through the trees like a scythe through standing wheat. They surveyed each tree as to height and placed in its original position on the model. A same scale model DC-8 could be placed in the swath, producing a vivid picture of airplane attitude. By matching damaged parts to specific trees, heading, pitch and slip could easily be determined. I could readily visualize what was going on in that cockpit, and it was awesome.

The DC-8 has flight spoilers on top of each wing, used to aid in turning. They only work if the landing gear is down. In this accident they never retracted him landing gear. Unfortunately, spoilers also destroy lift, create drag, and increase stall speed. The left hydraulic spoiler actuator was found in the fully extended position, positive proof the spoilers on the left wing were fully extended as the airplane contacted the trees. Spoilers are positively connected to actuators. Spoilers on the right wing were down. Which, in turn, proved the pilots were using full left aileron. This would be a normal reaction for a partially trained pilot. My knowledge of these peculiarities came about as the result of many years as a flight instructor on this airplane.

Before the coming of simulators all training was conducted in the airplane. The two engine landing maneuver in the airplane was a bitch. Three airplanes of other airlines were lost in training before FAA inspectors refused to observe the maneuver anymore. Instructors became solely responsible for approving student's proficiency, and signing the forms. Hundreds of executions increased familiarity with the maneuver, and taught me the effect of spoilers in relation to performance.

The big problem of the two engine landing was directional control. When power changes are made, an extremely strong leg is necessary to apply enough rudder pressure to maintain directional control. This encourages the pilot to use ailerons, which is the wrong thing to do.

With 35 degrees yoke travel, the flight spoilers on one side are deflected, causing loss of performance and increased stall speed. After landing gear is extended, forget a go-around.

To show this pitfall, I developed a demonstration that helped students understand and correct. Before attempting a two-engine landing, at a safe altitude, with the airplane in the takeoff configuration, using max power and leaving the gear down, an outboard throttle is closed. Use of rudder for directional control is emphasized. With very little use of ailerons, a slight climb is noted. Then rudder pressure is relaxed and more ailerons are used. This deflects the spoilers and a <u>loss</u> of altitude is noted. This was the condition and configuration of the Arrow Air DC-8 as it impacted the trees. The airplane in this configuration, and heavily loaded, is incapable of maintaining altitude. These pilots were probably not exposed to this type training. If they were not, I would not expect a better result.

Since the arrival of simulators, most training is given in the simulator. It is not the same as in the airplane. Simulators are programed according to airplane manufacturers' specifications. You should expect performance data to be shaded to enhance sales. Before we went to 100% simulator training, I negotiated an agreement regarding new captains. Besides the normal first 25 hours line flying with a check captain, the first 200 hours line flying must be accomplished with a copilot who has at least 500 hours in the airplane.

In this accident, they never raised the landing gear. The limitation section of the airplane manual states, "Landing gear retraction must be initiated within three seconds of liftoff. Required climb performance cannot be attained with the landing gear down." Much confirming testimony was given by experts about the airplane being able to meet second segment climb requirements. Second segment climb extends from gear retraction until all obstacles are cleared. It does not begin until landing gear is retracted. The aircraft never reached second segment climb.

In Ottawa all four engine drive shafts were displayed. Numbers 1,2, and 3 exhibited a severe twist, number 4 only a slight twist. This evidence was conspicuous even to a novice like me. For you jet engine illiterates--the turbine is at the rear of the engine and drives the compressor at the front end. A drive shaft connects them. When an engine developing power strikes the ground, such as in a crash, the front rotation stops first. The rear continues to produce power, at least for a millisecond. The connecting shaft is twisted or sometimes broken. All this means is that the #4 engine was not developing any appreciable power at the time of impact. However, the engine manufacture still failed to acknowledge that the engine was not producing power, and that was a primary cause of the crash.

If that wasn't enough proof, the bleed valve on number four engine was found in the open position. This is positive proof number four engine suffered a loss of power. Each engine has a bleed valve that opens to let air escape from N2, thus facilitating an engine start. It is a fully automatic system over which the pilot has no control. When the engine is running, the only time the valve is open is when the engine is developing very little or no power (such as idle RPM on the ground). This valve had leaves and branches inside. The bleed valves on engines number one, two, and three were closed.

This accident, like most, was caused by a combination of factors. The airplane was overloaded. Fourteen thousand pounds of freight was aboard that did not show on the weight forms. This caused the pilots to fly at a lower speed (V2) than required for safety. The flight data recorder registered a lift off speed of only one knot above buffet speed (speed at which the airplane begins to shake before a stall). Any airplane in a buffet is losing lift. The number four engine failed or power was reduced at a critical time. The pilots did not react properly, probably because they were not trained to do so. Can you expect a pilot to execute a maneuver better than that for which he was trained?

The 'straw that broke the camels back' was the fact that there was an unknown quantity of ice in the belly. Pilots for small outfits, like Arrow

Air, receive pressure to accept airplanes with malfunctions. They are paid less than half the salary of pilots flying for larger airlines. You usually get what you pay for.

The hazard of ice in the belly was discovered when EAL was still operating the DC-8/63. One of our airplanes, assigned to charter operations (the same type charter that Arrow Air enjoyed), was grounded in Germany. The captain had explained in the log book of sluggish performance and a tail heavy condition. After the airplane was ferried to Miami (in the summertime), it sat in a hangar for two days while maintenance struggled with the problem. Not until water began to leak from the belly, on the third day, was the mystery solved. This may have been the same airplane that crashed.

The potable water system (water for lavatories, drinking and coffee) had been leaking, and all the water accumulated in the belly where it turned to ice. There are ¼ inch drain holes in the belly to eliminate the water, but they are closed in flight. With in-flight outside air temperature ranging to -50C, the ice is super cooled. The system, with a 100-gallon storage tank in a heated area, is replenished every time an airplane lands, and no records are kept.

Examination of the Arrow Air log books revealed that the lost airplane had a leaking potable water system for months with not enough time on the ground for the ice to melt. After landing, with no ventilation, the temperature is very slow to change. This circumstance can add 800 pounds to each subsequent takeoff. I estimated the accumulated weight to be at least 20,000 pounds.

A year before, this aircraft had experienced a catastrophic engine failure while taking off at Casablanca, Morocco. Shrapnel type damage to the wings, flaps, fuselage and horizontal stabilizer occurred in the form of holes and dents. Damage was repaired with temporary patches. Permanent patches were never applied as required. Each patch reduces performance. Also, they were flying with an inoperative EGT (number 4 engine) which is required for dispatch. The right bogie trim cylinder was leaking, another no-go item. A fire shield in one baggage compartment was missing, also a no-go item. Check your minimum equipment list.

Pilots who previously flew the airplane testified that a power reduction on #4 engine was necessary to prevent the EGT from exceeding the red line. This was a positive sign the engine was on it's last legs. At this takeoff weight, coupled with a power loss, they were doomed.

Before the trial, I was privy to attend the deposition of the world's foremost bomb expert (Walter-- his last name escapes me). If you don't think he was the best, just ask him. During the questioning he was asked, "Do you think there might be someone, somewhere in the world that might know as much about this subject as you do?"

His answer was a quick and emphatic, "No."

Next question, "Israel has a lot of experience with bombs on airplanes. Do you think maybe someone over there might know as much as you do?"

Answer, "No. I taught everyone over there everything they know." His self-confidence was not misplaced. His qualifications included 20 years as US Army demolition expert, and 20 years as FAA Chief Investigator of aircraft accidents related to bombs. He said the explosion of a bomb leaves a fingerprint at least as dependable as that of a human.

"How many aircraft accidents have you investigated, pertaining to bombs?"

"All of them."

"How about Pan Am 102 over Lockabee?"

"Yes. I was in charge of that too."

I don't believe anyone in the world could match the knowledge and experience that Walter possessed. Of course, he knew there was no bomb.

In my deposition, I was asked the same question pertaining to knowledge of the DC-8. I refused to testify about what anyone else might, or might not, know.

I also attended the deposition given by Mr. Epstein. Mr. Epstein was the head man of the NASA Jet Propulsion Division, an author of many books on jet engines, as well as a professor at many of the larger universities. We went out to lunch, and he explained a 'rotor stall' pertaining to a jet engine. I had never heard of a rotor stall. The only jet engine stalls I ever encountered were momentary in nature. When a jet engine experiences a rotor stall, power is lost indefinitely. The rotor stall may be induced with excessive deterioration of fuel injection nozzles. He had examined the nozzles of the #4 engine of this airplane and found them to be eroded beyond limits.

There was some talk about the TV Court channel televising the trial, but the plans didn't work out. The trial was held in Miami, and I was the last witness for the plaintiffs. To establish my credentials as an expert witness on the DC-8, when asked what airplanes I was rated on, I forgot to mention all the Boeings. But after my qualifications were established, my nervousness subsided.

Early in the cross examination, I was asked to explain to the jury the definition of the FAA certified stall speed. Although the question was a surprise, it is a process I had been bitching about for years. I told the jury, "I guess the best way to define this would be to tell you how the FAA certified stall speed is arrived at." This is the gist of the message I tried to get across:

This test is performed in a new airplane, which will perform better than an old airplane, by test pilots who have practiced the maneuver to perfection. The stall speed is a very important number on which many other speeds are based, such as V2, the safety climb out speed. It is to the advantage of the manufacturer to get this number as low as possible. For example, if this speed on a B-747 can be reduced one knot, 10,000 pounds can be added to the landing weight. It is not necessary for a government inspector to observe this test. All observers may be employees of the manufacturer. This raises the question of conflict of interest.

In this test, at a safe altitude, the throttles are closed, and a predetermined rate of decrease in airspeed is attempted. The airplane begins to settle and lose airspeed. In the DC-8 the first warning of an impending stall is a mild buffet before the stall warning is activated. As airspeed decreases the stall warning shakes the yoke and makes a pretty loud clacking racket, which continues until the angle of attack is reduced. The sensor is a small vane under the right wing which senses angle of attack, much the same as you might find under the wing of small aircraft. As the speed further decreases, the buffet gets worse. It feels like you are sitting on the end of a stiff diving board with someone jumping up and down behind you. The next thing you know, the airplane is falling like a rock. Dirt and anything loose in the cockpit is flying around. If it wasn't for your seat belt, you would be flying too. This is not, repeat <u>not</u>, the certified stall speed. This is the 1-G stall speed. As airspeed continues to decrease, and the airplane continues to fall, takeoff power is applied and a recovery is initiated. The FAA certified stall speed is the lowest speed reached in the recover--a totally useless number to a pilot. The test is repeated with different aircraft configurations to establish stall speeds for specific configurations, but not all configurations. A method of postulation is used.

The FAA certified stall speed is always much lower than the actual 1-G stall speed. In this accident, the aircraft manufacturer admitted the airplane actually stalled at a speed 11 knots higher than the FAA certified stall speed, and this was without considering the airplane was in a bank, side-slipping with the spoilers deflected, and the increased weight from the ice in the belly. All of these conditions increase the speed at which a stall will occur. When certifying the B-727, altitude loss was recorded as 7000 feet.

Lawyers are not supposed to ask questions unless they know the answer. I think they made a mistake on this one. Most pilots flying today are not aware of this glaring misrepresentation, and it applies to all commercial airplanes. This is another example of how pilots are denied pertinent information. Don't expect to be given this kind of information by any training program. When a company receives a new airplane, the training program is set up to conform to manufactures specifications. Sometimes, it takes sworn testimony in a civil court to bring out the truth.

I was also asked the question, "How many times have you stalled this airplane?" Previous expert witnesses for the defense had answered, "Four or five". My answer was, after considering the hundreds of pilots trained, in the thousands.

After weeks of testimony, the case was settled in a sealed verdict awarding the plaintiffs large sums. The most unbelievable part of this whole thing is that neither the Canadian authorities, the NTSB, or the ALPA, are aware of the facts presented at this trial, or that a trial was ever held. I sent a copy of my findings to Mr. Batchelor, owner of Arrow Air. No acknowledgment was ever received. The ALPA did have tentative plans to test a DC-8 with ice on the wings, but that too never materialized.

It was determined from radio transmissions that the copilot probably made the takeoff. In an emergency such as this, you would expect the captain to take over control. In all probability, they were both on the controls. In any case, with the first few feet of altitude lost, the terrain warning system was activated with a loud computer generated voice, "PULL UP! PULL UP!" Volume increases until impact. Noise and vibration from the stall warning system added to the confusion. Sometimes, systems related to safety are a detraction. The airplane was shaking badly. Reading instruments was next to impossible. They bought the farm.

The CASB and the NTSB, when they issue their probable cause of an accident, are not always right. In the case of an airplane accident, the NTSB listens to testimony from witnesses who have a vested interest in the outcome. Deleterious information is withheld, and blame is pointed elsewhere. The age old notion of PYA (protect your ass) takes over. I remember one accident in Canada in which pilot error was declared the cause. For ten years the surviving relatives of the crew suffered unnecessary grief and harassment until ALPA proved a structural failure in the wing caused a wing to break off in flight.

Many people still believe the Arrow Air accident was caused by sabotage or ice on the wings. What a shame facts were never presented to the public. Don't let other people's mistakes ruin your career.

CHAPTER THREE
JET AIRPLANE INCIDENCES AND ACCIDENTS

~~~~~~

B-707/720/727/737 and DC-8

Northwest Airlines lost a B-707 in the Everglades. The pilots lost control at high altitude, and the airplane went straight in. I had a theory as to what might have caused the loss of control and spent many hours studying the flight control system. In maintenance I observed the assembling of the horizontal stabilizer movement system, and had lots of questions.

My theory: failure of the horizontal stabilizer jackscrew brake, was confirmed by discovery of the position of the stabilizer after the crash (jackscrew ball-nut assembly resting on structure). The pilots could not have put it there. Only aerodynamic force could have done so, and this would require a failure of one of the jackscrew brakes. Manual control of the stabilizer is limited by actuating cable movement. Main electric motor control is limited by electrical switches. Autopilot control is also limited by electrical switches. A Boeing test pilot agreed with my theory, but the NTSB, in the accident report, never mentioned this as a possible cause.

A Chicago newspaper reporting on a wrongful death civil lawsuit, resulting from the accident, revealed letters that indicated someone at Northwest and Boeing knew what would happen if this brake failed. Boeing and Northwest were fined one million dollars each in punitive damages. Sometimes, it takes sworn testimony in a court of law to find the truth.

I gave Eastern's Director of Training the newspaper article with the suggestion we train our pilots how to handle this type failure. He contacted Boeing, who denied everything. I was counseled not to discuss aerodynamic problems with students.

To understand how the horizontal stabilizer works, you should keep in mind certification requirements for static stability. Sometimes, safety regulations cause other problems. To carry passengers, the aircraft must past tests conducted through out the full speed envelope of the airplane. Purpose of this certification test is to insure that if an in-flight upset occurs, and no one at the controls, the airplane will not dive into the ground nor pitch up and stall. The test is accomplished while in level stabilized flight by simply pushing the yoke forward enough to upset level flight and let the airplane recover to level flight without pilot assistance.

This requirement is met by design of a horizontal stabilizer that carries a negative lift. As airspeed increases, negative lift on the stabilizer increases, causing the airplane to pitch up. Look closely, and you can see the inverted camber and angle of attack. As the nose comes up through horizontal, and airspeed decreases, negative stabilizer lift decreases. This allows the nose to once again drop below the horizon. The scenario is repeated with decreasing osculation until level flight is regained. Imagine a balance scale – put extra weight on one end and remove. The scale will return to normal. If the stabilizer ever carried a positive lift, you would do an outside loop, and there would be nothing you could do to prevent. Military aircraft are not required to pass commercial tests, and have totally different designs.

In level flight, when power is applied, airplanes tends to pitch up. I have had aeronautical engineers tell me this is caused by engine thrust line. This is not caused by thrust line of engines. It is caused by induced airflow around the horizontal stabilizer. Conversely, when power is reduced, the airplane tends to pitch down because induced airflow is reduced. A ground, test revealed, induced airflow from engine exhaust around the stabilizer to be in excess of 100MPH. In- flight, air flow around the stabilizer is increased in the same way. This is why the pitot head is always mounted in an area away from any induced airflow.

Inboard engines are more effective than outboard because they are nearer to the stabilizer.

The Boeing-707, 720 and 727 all use the same system for moving the horizontal stabilizer. There are actually three brakes on the jackscrew. The important one is the one that prevents reverse rotation. I made an in-flight test of all our 727's for stabilizer brake operation and found two in which an unwanted slippage could be induced. The brake assemblies were not changed because, "Could not duplicate on the ground." Of course maintenance could not duplicate. No way could they produce aerodynamic loads on the ground.

The stabilizer trim wheel in the cockpit is directly connected by cables coiled around a drum on the bottom of the jackscrew. One cannot move without the other. In training, all pilots were required to recover from a runaway stabilizer. At a high altitude an instructor would hold the pickle switch, either up or down, causing the main stabilizer motor to drive the stabilizer. The well trained student would quickly grab the trim wheel (causing a clutch on main electric motor to slip), and disengage the two stabilizer switches. This was usually followed by a jam stabilizer landing. Now the student thinks he is qualified to handle a runaway stabilizer. If this were true, a lot more people would be alive today. He has only learned how to handle an electrical malfunction. By grabbing the trim wheel. He is only slipping a clutch on the motor.

Since the horizontal stabilizer always carries a negative lift, and due to the location of the stabilizer pivot point (lift area aft of the pivot point is seven times greater that of the area forward of the pivot point), rotational pressure around the pivot point is transferred to the ball-nut assembly. Pressure is always up the jackscrew (less negative lift, airplane down). The jackscrew is so well designed and slippery, on the ground, weight of the elevators will lock brakes. In the case of a jackscrew brake failure (the one that prevents reverse rotation), as the ball nut begins to slide up the jackscrew, the drum begins to turn, the trim wheel spins, and the airplane begins to dive. Due to the size of the drum on the bottom of the jackscrew, and attachment to trim wheel, forces generated are in the magnitude of 100 to 1. No way can anyone stop this type runaway by grabbing the trim wheel. You would just break some fingers.

But, there is a way to recover. In a dive of this nature, the more back pressure on the yoke, the faster the runaway, resulting in a steeper dive. The electric motor is not strong enough to over come aerodynamic pressures. Inputs from the motor will be overcome by aerodynamic generated pressure. The clutch will slip if you use the pickle switch. Back pressure on the yoke increases upward pressure at the ball-nut assembly. This is due to rotational pressure around the stabilizer pivot point. When in a high speed dive, moving the yoke froward may seem nonsense able. But, that is the only way you will be able to use the stabilizer trim. Back pressure on the yoke must be released to mitigate upward pressure at the ball-nut. I like to compare the recovery with reeling in a big fish. The fishing method; when the fish is hooked, put lots of back pressure on the rod (yoke). Don't try to reel in. Drop the rod tip, which releases tension, and reel in (pickle switch) fast. Repeat until control is regained. You may have to use the pickle switch all the way to the ground.

Here is a simple test of the B-727 jackscrew brake, the one that prevents reverse rotation. You need to take someone along to hold the pedestal brake in the disengaged position. The pedestal brake was a later addition. It prevents opposite inputs to the stabilizer and elevator. Installed beneath the cockpit floor; it senses opposite movement of elevator and stabilizer cables, and seizures both cables. Expect a loud ratchet sound when it engages. It is made of light material and designed to only slip the clutch on the main stabilizer electric motor. No way is it effective enough to stop aerodynamic ball nut assembly slippage. The release knob is located on the floor by the copilot's seat.

In level flight, use pickle switch to trim airplane nose up (this moves the stabilizer nose down increasing negative lift), and hold level flight with forward pressure on the yoke. This creates the famous Z (elevator tab goes up, elevator goes down forming a Z in relation to the stabilizer). Now you have increased upward pressure on the trailing edge of the stabilizer, stemming from elevator lift. This pressure is transferred around the stabilizer pivot point (located on the main spar) to the ball nut assembly on the jackscrew, which is forward of stabilizer pivot point. Visualize an unbalanced see saw. One end goes up and the other down. Leverage can be magnified by location of the pivot point. In the absence of a jackscrew brake, the ball nut assemble will slowly slide down the jackscrew (increasing negative lift) causing the trim wheel to turn, increasing magnitude of dive. Boeing never recognized this problem.

As OAT chairman, I ask Boeing for data on horizontal stabilizer negative lift. My question was to ascertain how much pressure the ball nut sustained in normal flight. My letter was never answered. We should have had better operational information on the tail of that airplane. Trouble is, I don't think Boeing had, or has, accurate information. We lost one in South America against the side of a mountain. The cause was never established. A 727 crashed into a mountain in Japan. The horizontal stabilizer jackscrew ball-nut assembly was found at the extreme position, same as the one in the Everglades. It had passed all the stops and was resting on structure. A position it could reach only with a brake failure. An order was drawn by the FAA to ground all 727s. The order was never implemented. Nor was this information processed. Makes you wonder about politics.

DC-8 airplanes use a totally different system for stabilizer control, thus eliminating the above problem. However, the airplane would not pass the static stability test. It passed at the lower MACH numbers. But at higher numbers, it did not pass static stability tests. A high speed decent would not stop without pilots inputs. Airspeed would increase until you were going straight down. Center of lift, on top of wings, moved aft and the stabilizer provided not enough negative lift. More negative lift equals more drag. Thus, a pitch trim compensator was added.

The pitch trim compensator (PTC) system senses airspeed from the copilots pitot system. At high speeds, an electrical signal is sent to a spring on the bottom of the yoke beneath the cockpit floor on the copilot's side. The higher the airspeed, the more back pressure exerted on the yoke. The system is controlled by a three position switch on the console – on, off, and test. The test mode applies back pressure to the yoke of up th 35 pounds, which can be easily overcome (a pre-flight check). An indicator, that looks like a worm, on the copilots yoke tells how much back pressure is exerted on the yoke. In case of a jammed stabilizer landing, the test position was used to help pilots raise the nose. Simply use test switch until desired back pressure is attained. Then place switch if off position. This relieved the pilot from holding constant back pressure.

The DC-8 stabilizer is moved by hydraulic energy, through a system of chains and sprockets. The stabilizer is locked in position until hydraulic pressure is directed to a check valve that only opens above 1000 pounds pressure. Then 3000 pounds pressure is available to up or down actuators. Without hydraulic pressure, manual trim is available. If there is any mechanical failure or breakage, the stabilizer simply jams, and stays where it was.

There are two tabs on the elevator. The inboard tab is the control tab, placed inboard because it is the last to stall. The outboard one is the stabilizer tab. It is geared to the stabilizer, designed to cause the elevator to trail the stabilizer, thus eliminating the Z and reducing drag. I don't know how well it worked. Another airline flew an airplane for at least two weeks with that tab missing. Pilots didn't notice the difference. Someone on the ground happened to look at the elevator. Boeing aircraft have the same two elevator tabs, supposedly with the same functions. But their positions are reversed – inboard/outboard. Figure that one out.

This happened while giving a line check, ATL to LAX, in a Flying Tiger DC-8/63: I was flying from the right seat. The aircraft required four degrees right rudder trim. In order to properly check rigging, I shutoff hydraulic pressure. Movement of the stabilizer caused the right rudder peddle moved appreciable, slamming me against the copilots window. The two systems are fully independent – not connected in any way. At a loss to understand what was happening, I repeated the action with the same results.

My writeup in the log book was detailed. The next morning I checked with maintenance to see what happened. The airplane was gone, with no corrective action. On the ground at ATL, with no engines running, I had the engineer go to the cockpit, turn on the aux pump, shutoff hydraulic pressure to the rudder and actuate the pickle switch. All this, as I stood under the tail and watched the rudder swing to the right. Needless to say, I was shocked.

The next morning, in Miami I wrote a letter and hand delivered it to the FAA. While I was there, the incident was reported to Washington.

There is only one hydraulic return line that returns fluid to the reservoir -- from both stabilizer and rudder. A check valve is required to prevent a pressure from one to reach the other. The DC-8/63 manual did not show a check valve. All other manuals displayed the check valve. In the end, nothing came of this.

A DC-8/63, taking off from Kennedy crashed. The track followed what you would expect from an unwanted rudder deflection. The rudder boost lever was found in the off position.

Two B-737 aircraft were lost with fatalities to all on board. While a definitive cause has not been forthcoming, investigators believe a hard over rudder movement might have occurred. Not being qualified on the B-737, maybe I shouldn't comment, but here goes anyway.

All of our four engine Boeing jets, and the B-737, had the same basic compass and auto pilot system. The auto pilot does not supply any signal to the rudder, the yaw damper does that. Directional control is accomplished with electronic signals to the ailerons. A hard-over signal to the ailerons will produce the same deadly maneuver that occurred in both accidents. I defy anyone to distinguish, with the old-fashioned flight data recorder, between a hard over rudder and a hard over aileron.

The auto pilot system provides protection against hard over signals by limiting roll rate and maximum degree of bank. However, the magnitude of these protections are different, and provided only through the mode selector. Different roll rates and bank are automatically selected, depending on the position of the mode selector. If a directional signal is received by the auto pilot that does not go through the mode selector, there will be <u>no</u> restriction on roll rate or degree of bank, and a hard over signal to the ailerons will take place.

On our Boeings it was possible to mechanically demonstrate in-flight, which I did many times. On the B-720, with the Captain flying on auto pilot with the flight director in heading mode, if the copilot synched his RMDI (which he was supposed to do if it is out of sync), a signal is sent to the ailerons that bypassed the mode selector, producing a hard over unrestricted aileron maneuver. It is a violent maneuver.

When I first saw, on TV, the video simulation of one of the accidents, I said to my wife, "That's the same maneuver I demonstrated 25 years ago."

Since the accidents, US Air aircraft have been modified. The sync knob had been replaced with an electronic synching system. Any electronic interference in this new system may bypass the mode selector and causes a hard over signal to the ailerons. Electronic interference can come from anywhere. There are many sources of electronic interference other than transmission lines.

This happened to Air Force Blackhawk helicopters. Three or four of them were lost before the cause was found to be electronic interference from power lines which caused the auto pilot to produced a hard over signal. The fix was to install lead shields around the electronics. The real sadness is the fact that lifesaving information is not decimated. I contacted the FAA and NTSB, but they didn't want to talk. I realize newer airplanes have different systems. The old systems were new once upon a time.

An Eastern DC-8 flown by Captain Robins, one of my students, lost all four engines at 24,000 feet over California. He was descending at low speed, with the throttles closed. When leveling off, engines did not respond to the throttles. Fifteen thousand feet was lost before an engine responded to the throttle. You can imagine the chaos that was taking place in the cockpit while they were trying to restart.

Many meetings were held to determine the cause, without success. Everyone thought the engines were not running. Attempts to restart were rehashed. Not until someone at a later meeting asked Robbie if the EGT deteriorated when the start lever was placed in the off position, did we learn what happened. His answer, "Yes", opened the understanding of what had happened. The engines were still running. His airspeed was so low, N2 RPM dropped so low, (due to the reduced idle setting), the fuel controls lost the throttle senses and assumed a low idle condition. When this happens, fuel control will not sense throttle position. It's like the throttles are disconnected. All you can do is increase airspeed, thus increasing N2 RPM, and hope for the best. To save fuel, someone had reset the adjustment to a lower idle. Jet engines have an idle adjustment similar to that on your car. In Robie's case, his airspeed dropped so low, N2 RPM dropped low enough to drop the throttles out of the loop.

You can prove this on the ground by starting an engine with the throttle full forward. The engine will start normally. Only when N2 RPM reaches the preset value, will the engine respond normally. In the simulator, when the engine does not respond to throttle, it is called a hung start – always low RPM.

As a result of all this, a restriction was placed in the limitation section of the airplane manual. Minimum N2 RPM for flight was always a question on oral examinations. Thirty years later I was informed by

ALPA engineers that this limitation does not appear in manuals today. A lesson learned, and not passed on, may have to be relearned.

All jet engines have a maximum time limitation to spool up. On some, anything below six seconds is acceptable. In a normal descent with throttles closed, don't be surprised if the engines don't respond immediately. Six seconds is enough time to set off panic.

CHAPTER FOUR
PROP AIRPLANE INCIDENTS

Some things I learned about aircraft I have flown were learned from instruction, and some were from curiosity or necessity. All were of value. I know some of these airplanes are no longer around. But, some of the systems are. Methods of discovery don't change. If you don't know the mistakes we made in dealing with these incidents, you may be prone to repeat.

DC-3------Commercial version of Army Air Corps C-47

After the defeat of Germany in World War Two, the largest airline in the world was put together to fly Soldiers home over the southern Atlantic route. Troops boarded airplanes in Europe. Crew consisted of pilot and copilot only. Pilots flew only one leg of the journey. The first leg was to Africa, second to Natal, Brazil, third to Belem, Brazil, fourth to Trinidad, fifth to Miami. Crews were changed at each stop. Soldiers were allowed to deplane only for the length of time it took to refuel – kinda like the pony express. Airplanes returned empty. The project, named "Green Project", was a huge success, with over 100 arrivals per day in Miami.

Flying between Belem and Natal, Brazil was direct, long and lonely. Over nothing but jungle, no roads or towns. The only place a survivable landing could be made was in a river. So, passing over every river I noted the time. In case we had to land, it might help to know the nearest river. There were no check points, radios, or navigational aids.

On one return flight to Natal, with just the copilot and myself on board, I almost fell out of the airplane. While the copilot was flying, without saying a word, I left the cockpit to relieve myself. Most of the aircraft had a makeshift toilet in the rear, but this one had no facilities at all. I found an empty cardboard lunch box and defecated therein.

Determined to throw out the mess, I tried to open the rear cargo door, but with no success. There were two over-wing emergency exits, one over each wing. The plug-type doors, about two feet wide and four feet high, located over the wing in a negative pressure area. All you had to do to open the exit was turn the handle. Negative pressure was supposed to pulled it outward. Well, this one was stuck. The handle would turn, but the door would not budge. I pounded and kicked it, even considered using the fire ax to chop a hole in the fuselage. My morale was not too high, nor was my thought process.

When the emergency exit door finally popped out; I had such a grip on the handle, it took me with it. My body exited the airplane so far I saw the tail wheel. I have no memory of climbing back in, but the next day I had bruises on the outside of my legs from the knees to the hips.

Had I not been able to climb back in, my death, without a doubt, would have been reckoned a suicide. Today when I read of a suicide, I have doubts. Maybe it could have been an accident. For a few weeks nightmares painted a vivid picture of that tail wheel. After an accident, don't assume anything as absolute, unless you were there. Landing at Natal, the tower advised that we had a large hole in the fuselage. I wrote in the log book, emergency exit left side missing, and no crapper.

At Eastern, our DC-3s were on the block to be sold. Flying copilot with Walt Hill, testing a DC-3 after a double engine change, we discovered that with the left engine shut down the aircraft could not maintain altitude. Looking around, we observed that the deicer boots on both wings appeared to be inflated. This caused a considerable loss of lift. The deicer boot is a rubber covering of the leading edge of the wing. When ice forms, air is pumped through veins expanding the boot, thus breaking and shedding the ice.

A new lightweight boot was in the process of being installed on our DC-3s. The new boot, being soft, required vacuum pressure to deflate and cling to the leading edge. Without vacuum, at high angles of attack, lift was decreased by destroying the contour of the leading edge of the wing.

Both engines had vacuum pumps, but only the left one was used for deflating the boots. With an inoperative left engine, no vacuum was available to deflate the boots and as a result, you were going down.

After a couple of weeks no corrective action had been taken, nor pilots advised, I told Fred Davis (Fred was in charge of engineering) of my concern. He said, a "T" had been installed in the vacuum line to allow the pump on either side to be used for boot deflation. Only half of the fleet had been modified. The half not yet modified would be sold first, as is. Simply put, any airplane, not yet modified, that lost the left engine would probably crash. I thought this to be a serious breach of safety and common sense. An example of the profit motive.

While having lunch one day in the old company cafeteria, next to the small maintenance hangar, I sat with Mr. Van Mensill, the CAA maintenance inspector assigned to EAL. I told him about the deicer boots. I did so without any motive or any idea of what would happen. The CAA (forerunner of FAA) grounded all our DC-3s not yet modified until the "T" was installed. Which cost the company lots of money. For reporting the incident, my relationship with company officers took a huge hit. For this, I am not regretful. You can't always depend on others to boost safety.

Some DC-3s had flotation tanks in the wings (information not widely known). This information came to me while cleaning the aircraft. Airtight compartments in the wings had vent tubes that terminated in the cabin. A little panel on both cabin side walls, when opened, displayed the tubes with cork stoppers for plugging. I guess that's why they floated so long after a ditching. One that made a water landing off the coast of South America, floated so long, the Navy was dispatched to sink it.

Early DC-3s were equipped with a steam heaters, which could only operate in-flight. They were replaced with gasoline heaters. Before the new heaters, in the winter time, after gear retraction – on DC-2s the gear had to be raised with a hand pump – the copilot had to leave the cockpit and get the heater going. That was quite a chore, garbed in heavy overcoat and gloves.

The new gas heaters required an outside air scoop, which was installed just aft of the copilots window. In the early days, it was common practice to discard paper coffee cups and other debris out the cockpit windows. The first debris thrown out the copilots window went into the scoop and caused a heater fire. It didn't take long to relocate the scoop. You would think engineers would have more forethought. When equipment is added or changed, pilots beware. One captain would stick his head out the window. He said to blow away dandruff.

Our DC-3s had a small passenger loading-door at the rear of the cabin on the left side that had steps attached which automatically extended when the door was opened. After landing at La Guardia, as soon as the stairs hit the ground, a young woman, buck naked, rushed down the stairs, and began to prance around in a foot of snow. From the right seat I couldn't see a thing. The captain, acted like he had never seen a naked woman before. I know I hadn't, at least not in the snow. He was leaning out his side window to get a better view. Occasionally he would withdraw his head and give me a description of what was going on. A policeman was chasing the naked woman around in the snow. He finally caught her, put his overcoat around her and led her away. She had undressed in the lavatory, located near the door, just before landing, and was first to scamper down the steps. The lesson here, might be more about people than airplanes. Fly passengers long enough, and you will have some weird ones.

DC-4

The cockpits were not waterproof. They leaked so much, canvas covers in the cockpit were provided for pilots to shield themselves from rain. A cheap way to fix leaks. It was really difficulty to make an instrument approach with canvas draped around and everything in the cockpit wet. In cold weather, there was a problem of staying warm.

In order to shorten the landing roll, it was found the following procedure to be quite effective. After landing, with nose wheel on the ground, as brakes are applied, and nose gear oleo strut is compressed, put as much back pressure on the yoke as you can without raising the nose. This deflected the elevator upward creating more drag and a downward pressure on the empennage. Downward pressure increases the weight of the aircraft without increasing momentum. The procedure worked well on later Douglas aircraft as well as the Constellation. But, if you let the nose come up, you will blow tires. I am not suggesting you try any of these procedures on newer airplanes. But, the theory may be applicable to most aircraft. Any knowledge is good knowledge. I observed two Captains blow tires learning to use this method.

We lost a DC-4 over Maryland. From level flight, at 6000 feet, he just nosed over and went straight in. Cause of the accident was never determined. Some investigators believed the pilots, either purposely or accidentally, engaged the gust lock. The gust lock is a mechanism that locks the elevator and aileron, used on the ground to prevent wind damage. The system is operated by a large lever latched to the floor. It takes some strength and deliberate action to engage. To engaged accidently is not plausible.

Joe Toth, the EAL test pilot, had a theory that was never mentioned in the investigation. His premise was that one of the elevator trim tab cables could have broken. The tab has two cables from the tail to the control in the cockpit. Both cables are spring loaded, stretched by a tensor that exerts a continuous pull to prevent slack. Joe's theory was that if one cable broke, the other cable would be jerked, deflecting the tab to an extreme position. Also, one tensor may have become disengaged from structure.

We ran a test on an aircraft in the hanger. One cable was cut. The tab was yanked to the extreme position, thus giving credence the theory.

Plans were made to test an airplane in flight. The Navy had an old DC-4 which they agreed to let us use. Joe was to be the Captain and I would be the only other person aboard. Joe's scheme was, when I cut the cable, if and when, the airplane went into a dive, he would roll it over to the inverted position, and let the airspeed deteriorate. At a lower airspeed, he would gain control with the yoke alone. The company was going to pay us both $1500 extra. My requirements were; furnish me with a parachute, remove aft cargo door, and all loose stuff. No one would tell me when to jump. I suppose they intended to cut a hole in the cabin floor for access. The test was never staged. At least one more DC-4 was lost in similar circumstances.

My wife knew I was engaged in flying test hops. When she realized we didn't wear parachutes, she had something like a cat fit.

Eastern had an interchange agreement with other airline which required pilots of both airlines to fly the equipment of the other. Cockpit layouts were different. On our DC-4s two similar handles were located between the pilots. The left one was the flap handle and the right one was the landing gear handle. On the interchange aircraft the handle positions were reversed. It didn't take a genius to figure out that sooner or later someone would grab the wrong handle. The landing gear handle had a wheel on the end as a reminder. The flap handle had a knob on the end, the shape of a flap. That's not enough to overcome habit.

Some pilots, on the landing roll, liked to retract the wing flaps. The thought being, increased weight on the landing gear would provide better braking. A DC-4 flown by Captain Andy McDonough experienced landing gear collapse on the landing rollout. Some time later I walked up behind Andy while he was standing at a hotel bar, slapped him on the shoulder, and said, "How fast were you going when you pulled the gear handle up?"

"About sevent.... Oh, I didn't do that," was his too quick reply. We both laughed. Habit can get you in lots of trouble.

DC-6/7s-----One memory that sticks in mind.

The company wanted me to instruct on the DC-7, but I didn't have much experience on the airplane and thought it would not be fair to the students. Soon I began to feel the pressure. "You have no choice," I was told. I relented and said "OK."

Immediately I was informed, "Your first students are in Atlanta tomorrow morning at four o'clock." I grabbed an airplane manual and read it on the way to Atlanta. I hadn't flown the aircraft in some time and felt shaky about the arrangement. My qualification was on paper only. If you think a license makes any difference, when you get in trouble, paste it on the windshield, and see if it makes any difference. Blind leading the blind is never good.

Arriving at midnight, I waited until 4:00 a.m. for my students. Captains Henry Holder and Andy Andrews arrived on time. A certain number of night landings were required, and due to scheduling this would be the only period in which to get them. There was not a lot of time for briefing, but I did tell them, "Don't use the brakes. You will blow the tires." This was the first time either had seen the cockpit. Simulators were still in the future.

Starting students with night landings I knew was not the best way to begin, but again there was no choice. Andy took the left seat first and completed his required landings. Then Henry moved to the left seat. His landings were not the best, but at least he didn't break anything. Not until the last one.

We had to make only one more landing to satisfy requirements. The one with a simulated engine failure. It was starting to get light now, but this last landing would be counted as a night landing. Henry touched down hard and fast. Using full reverse power on all engines, the engines suffered an over speed, and we were headed for the boondocks. Both tires on the left side blew, and I had a handful of airplane. I was lucky to keep it on the runway. We called maintenance and left the airplane sitting on the runway.

Two engines had to be changed due to over speed. The engine over speed was my fault. I should never have let the RPM get that high. But no one ever mentioned the oversight to me. More proficiency on my part could have saved the day.

Two other instructors and myself worked with Henry everyday for a week, until the company called a halt. Henry and Andy went up for their rating ride together. Henry passed and Andy failed. Maybe we concentrated too much on the weaker student. Learning from rote may not be the best way. In any case, Henry failed his first proficiency check and never flew the airplane again. Andy repeated the check, and flew the airplane until retirement.

While we were still operating from the old 36th Street terminal in Miami, Thad Royal came taxiing to the gate in a DC-7. He experienced a brake failure and collided with a parked Constellation. A fire erupted that consumed the Constellation. No one was injured.

The next morning when the FAA arrived to investigate the accident, the first question asked was, "Who was flying the airplane?". When told it was Thad Royal, the response was, "Oh yeah. He's the guy who landed the DC-3 in a cow pasture." The response was as if Thad was a weak pilot, when in fact he did a magnificent job in landing the airplane in a cow pasture with both engines inoperative. After an accident, there will always be too much effort toward placing the blame. Pilots are first choice. The longer an investigation goes on, probability of discovering the truth is enhanced.

The investigation turned up a flex line in the brake system with a small hole that caused the failure. The FAA contended the hole was not large enough to cause an immediate brake failure, and that Thad had plenty of time to stop, unless he was taxiing too fast.

A meeting was held in the hydraulic shop to determine the nature of the accident. Thad asked me to attend as his representative. The flex line with the hole in it was attached to a hydraulic machine to simulate conditions at the time of the accident. Time to pump all the fluid through the small hole was about five minutes. "See, I told you, he had plenty of time to stop!", exclaimed the FAA agent.

Near the end of the meeting, when asked for my comments, I said, "During the whole test the hydraulic pressure never exceeded 600 pounds (normal pressure is 3000 pounds). The de- booster, at the brake assembly, reduced the pressure to nothing and he had an instantaneous brake failure." The FAA representative tried to rebut my explanation, but without success. My experience tells me, after an accident or incident, the FAA is out to get you. Newer airplanes may still use brake de-boosters. Does yours?

An actual test in an airplane was also conducted on the emergency air brake system. From the time of emergency brake handle actuation until actual brake application was so long it would have been useless. Thad clearly had insufficient time to stop the airplane, and he was exonerated. Don't hesitate to get technical help when needed.

Charlie Martykan was another student who left me with memories. His favorite saying, "Nobody can think and fly at the same time" (he pronounced it 'Tink', with a slight Polish accent). Which exemplified his whole being. I trained him in other airplanes and earned my pay each time.

Marty, as we called him, called from Chicago, saying, "Clyde, I'm in trouble. Can you help me?" Lost in an area of thunderstorms at night, he had landed at Waterloo, Iowa, a few hundred miles off course. No high octane fuel was available, so, with his own money, he bought 1200 gallons of 100 octane gasoline(we used a higher octane). Had he taken off using this fuel, the engines would probably failed. Someone had the presence of mind to put the 100 octane in tanks not used for takeoff, and tell him to use it only in cruise. Sometimes you are not aware of your own misfortune. Who said, "What you don't know won't hurt you?"

After the storms passed Marty headed for Chicago, and a not-so-cordial welcome from Chief Pilot Blanchard. The result of all this was a letter in Marty's file which said in effect, "Screw up again and you are out of here."

All airlines keep a file on pilots. I have heard some airlines keep two files. I don't know this to be true. In case of a law suite, bad things in a file can be costly. My file was devoid of many complimentary letters, of which I had copies. I don't know if this was sloppy bookkeeping or intentional.

National Airlines lost a DC-7 in the Gulf of Mexico. 'Red Stettner', the copilot, had below average remarks in his file. Because of this, a wrongful death suit cost someone lots of money. We purged our records to eliminate below average grades. I flew with some, and re-rated them.

Constellation L-749--------1049

The Lockheed Constellation was a four-engine prop airplane with three vertical fins and rudders. The first models carried 75 passengers from Miami to New York in four hours, our first pressurized airplane.

An overjealous cleaner attempting to service the master can while the engines were running, didn't know the airplane was pressurized for a ground pressurization check. When he released the latch, the can came out like a shot from a cannon, hit the ground and literally exploded. The contents covered the cleaner and anything else within 50 feet. This was before self-contained toilets. And I thought varsol smelled bad.

One problem with the airplane, in cruise, the tail tended to slide from side to side. This could be corrected by skillful cross trimming. Our method of leveling the turn and bank indicator was deficient. Like all reciprocating engines, the mag check had to be performed before every takeoff. Runup was prohibited unless wing flaps were extended. The reason; without flaps extended, the tail, with three vertical stabilizers, shook so bad, damage could occur.

When flight testing the L-749, after multiple engine changes, it was normal to shut down and feather (turn the propeller blades into the wind to prevent rotation) the props on three engines at a time. With only one engine running, and with the use of a gadget that measured frequency vibration, it was possible to pinpoint where the vibration was coming from. Different parts of an engine produce different frequencies of vibration.

One day I was flying from the right seat with only one engine running, Joe said, "I wonder what the glide ratio is?" And with that, he shut down the last engine with the mixture control. I had been descending quite rapidly with only one engine running. Now we came down like a rock. Over Opa Locka at ten thousand feet, it is doubtful that we could have made it to MIA. Bill Hagen, our flight engineer, was more than a little upset and began to un-feather the props (without any prompting), rapidly. Bill was one of my favorites. He was killed in an automobile accident between the Chicago airport and the hotel during a layover. Pilots should recognize where real danger exists.

A Constellation, in flight, experienced severe vibration, and the captain elected to make an emergency landing. Luckily, no one was killed. The cause of the vibration was failure of the hydraulic access door latch, located on top of the left stub wing. The door, in a lift area, flapping up and down, caused the vibration. Joe and I had previously made a test flight with this door open and reported severe vibration that could be eliminated with use of takeoff flaps. The pilots were never made aware, in a timely manner, of this information.

One of the early L-749s up near St. Augustine, Florida threw a prop blade which came right through the fuselage, causing one fatality. Dick Merrill, riding the jump seat, took over the controls and made an emergency landing. Dick was our most famous pilot. His career dated back to the time of airmail pilots. That model L-749 had hollow prop blades, and was certified to climb only with wing flaps extended. They were climbing without flaps, which was never mentioned in the investigation.

This was our first airplane with reversible props. Pilots were concerned with possible in-flight reversal. We made jury rig to bypass the safety switch on the right main landing gear oleo strut. We called it the squat switch. It's purpose was to prevent in-flight reversal as well as other functions.

We made a test of in-flight reversal on a #3 prop. It was accomplished with the throttle closed. Yaw was easily controlled. Adding power caused somewhat of a problem, and vibration was severe. My assessment of the test was to the effect, it proved nothing. If a prop goes into reverse while the engine is developing power, I think, as it goes through flat pitch, the blades will be thrown right out of the hub. In flight reversal should not be a cause for worry. Centrifugal forces keep the blades in forward thrust position. Transfer of oil pressure in the prop dome is necessary to force blades to reverse. That would require a major mechanical mishap.

The Constellation was a hydraulic nightmare with hydraulic flight controls and manual reversion mechanism for flight controls. The system was not proficient in elevator control. Hence, an electrical method was incorporated. An electric motor used, used only in an emergency, to move the elevator was protected by a non trip-free circuit breaker. A non trip free circuit breaker is one that when held in, will still make contact, even though the malfunction still exists. After many years of operation, without pilot notification, a trip-free circuit breaker was installed in this circuit. A trip free circuit breaker is one that cannot be reset until the fault is corrected. Someone with jurisdiction saw fit to change regulations. Only trip free circuit breakers were allowed in any circuit. Only a few flight engineers were aware of the change, and no one was aware of the location. If a pilot activated this system, and encountered a short circuit, the elevators would be locked. No use trying to hold a circuit breaker in. It won't make contact.

The HF radio transmitter was located just behind the captain's seat with a long lead up to the ceiling. When the transmitter was activated, an electrical field was generated that affected the surrounding area. Any place in the cockpit; you could hold a flourescent bulb in your hand, transmit on HF, and the bulb would light up. All kinds of tricks were forthcoming. When the stewardess came to the cockpit with coffee,

I would ask her to hold the bulb to her left temple, and tell her if she told a lie, the bulb would light up. After a couple of trivial questions, I would ask, "Did you have sex last night?" No matter the answer, I would transmit. The illuminated bulb would go sailing across the cockpit, usually accompanied by a scream.

Here is a story taken from my autobiography.

While instructing on the Constellation, Captain Chuck White, based in New Orleans, came to Miami for training. Having trained Chuck of other airplanes, it was a pleasure to be paired with him again. Chuck was a B-24 bomber pilot during the war, so stepping up to four engines was easy. He had a son playing little league football. So did I. He visited my home, and together we watched the little leaguers practice football. After finishing his training, he had a few days to wait for his check ride. I had returned to training flight engineers. With a flight engineer instructor to take care of the students, I had an airplane to play with. I asked Chuck if he would like to go along for the ride, and he jumped at the chance. During his training, Chuck had shown an unusual interest in boost-out work (flying without hydraulic flight controls). Flying without hydraulic controls in this airplane is possible, but just barely. It takes tremendous strength, and even then the airplane reacts very slowly.

Out over the ocean off Key Largo, we were on top of a flat overcast. The clouds below looked like a flat snow-covered prairie. Chuck was flying from the left seat. I had him descend so as to just skim along the top of the clouds. At this point I set his altimeter at zero. Now we could simulate the top of the overcast as the ground. I took over the controls, climbed to 1500 feet above the clouds and failed all hydraulic flight controls.

From the right seat, with my feet off the rudder pedals, and never touching the yoke, I demonstrated an approach and simulated landing on top of the clouds using engine power exclusively for control. Using the outboard engines for direction, the inboard for pitch and small adjustments on all engines for climb and descent, it is possible to make a controlled approach. A quick burst of power on the in boards just before landing, brought the nose up as effectively as the elevators. Chuck practiced three of four of these simulated landings and became quite proficient. So proficient that the last approach was made with an engine shut down.

On December 4, 1965, Chuck was flying Eastern Flight 853. Over New Jersey his Constellation collided with a Boeing 707. The Boeing landed at Idlewild Airport with 25 feet of one wing missing. Chuck's airplane suffered extensive damage that rendered all flight controls inoperative. It was getting dark, but there was still enough light for Chuck to spot an open area at the foot of Hunt's Mountain.

With the use of engine power, he maneuvered the airplane to the open spot and just before touchdown, raised the nose with a blast of power. The airplane slid along the ground, shedding both wings. When the fuselage came to rest, all the passengers escaped except three. This information came from the copilot, who survived.

When Chuck realized all the passengers were not accounted for, he entered the fuselage. While trying to help a soldier, still strapped in his seat, an explosion occurred. Chuck lost his life trying to help one more, after saving so many. A bronze plaque commemorating Chuck's skill and heroism stands at the foot of Hunt's Mountain.

Chuck was the only student whom I ever gave this type of training. I have never heard another instructor speak of doing it either. I don't believe there was another pilot in the world as well prepared to handle that emergency as was Chuck.

I don't believe in predestination, but I've often wondered why I gave him that training. Was it destiny or was it by chance? In any case, as Paul Harvey would say, "Now you have heard, "THE REST OF THE STORY".

When training flight engineers, with no copilot, I took my son along as copilot. After a week, he could takeoff, land, and do steep turns without any help. My son, still in highschool, had only a student license. He said, "Dad, I'm not going to put this in my log book."

When asked why, he replied, "No one would believe it."

You would never be able to get away with something like this today.

Martin 404

The M-404 was a remake of the M202, which had a weak wing --one broke off in flight–, and poor stability. With a beefed up wing and too much positive dihedral (wings angled upward), aileron control was insufficient. The correction was the addition of hydraulic powered ailerons to facilitate turning. When landing with full flaps, elevator control was inadequate, so a variable pitch stabilizer had to be added. The right propeller ground clearance was such that when the right main wheel tires went flat, the prop hit the ground. This didn't happen on the left side due to centrifugal force produced by prop rotation. To correct this, spacers were installed in the bottom of the right engine mounts, which raised the thrust line on the right engine, which in turn caused a power loss due to disturbed air entering the carburetor air scoop. This also caused the airplane to fly as if left wing heavy. Power on the right engine could be regained on that engine with extension of wing flaps, which changed the angle of attack. This was the only airplane I've ever flown that performed better with wing flaps down than with them up. Every M-404 we had cruised with three or four degrees right wing down trim. I wonder how much that cost the company over the life of the airplanes.

The ALPA asked me to investigate maintenance inspection practices pertaining to the center section of the M-404. Why they were interested, I don't remember. I spent half a day talking with mechanics on the hangar floor. Long since, I had learned the best information comes from those who do the work. There were two Martins that had been so shoddily repaired that the mechanics would not let their families ride on them. This fear probably came from the accident of a M-202 when a wing broke off in flight.

A close investigation of the paperwork on one of them revealed that a major crack in the main wing spar had been improperly repaired. An FAA inspector had refused to approve the work. The foreman agreed. Another inspector was called, and he too turned down the work with a note, "Improperly repaired." Without further work, the repair was finally approved by an engineer who had no authority to do so. He didn't even have a mechanic's airplane and engine license, much less inspector status. This was a profound violation of Federal Air Regulations. I called the ALPA with this information, advising them I had names, dates and numbers if they wanted them. I was told, "Forget it. If the FAA got hold of this, the fine might bankrupt the company." Sometimes economics overrides safety.

When the airplane was new, we had too many engine failures. On short hauls, we didn't bother to manually lean the mixture. When the mixture control was placed in auto lean, fuel mixture was at best power (hottest). We had 30 in-flight failures in two months before identifying the problem.

I'll say one good thing about the airplane, it had an air conditioner that could make snow in the cabin. It was an air to air conditioner with a huge compressor driven by the right engine. It required so much energy, if you lost the left engine, flight could not be sustained with the compressor running.

The compressor had a large oil tank that had to be serviced periodically. On the flight line I observed a mechanic on a ladder holding the hose nozzle from an oil truck, filling the tank. From time to time he would remove the nozzle from the tank, look down in the opening, then resume the task. There was no compressor installed on this airplane and the oil was making a big puddle on the ground. From a distance, hollering and waving my arms, I got his attention.

Eastern conducted takeoff tests at maximum gross weight and found that with an engine failure during takeoff the aircraft could not meet the required climb performance, although the CAA had certified that it would. The test caused a permanent reduction in maximum takeoff gross weight for Eastern only. The other airlines accepted the manufacturer's data.

We almost lost one due to faulty electrical design. On an approach to one of the New York airports, the pilots lost all the flight instruments. The engineers had designed a system that grounded all electrical flight instruments (both sides) to the same block. When the block became detached from the aircraft frame, all flight instruments were lost. Eastern modified the fleet to correct the problem. I previously thought the aeronautical engineers that designed these airplanes were so much smarter than I, they must have a reason for each particular design, but not anymore. I am still learning. Now, I am trying to learn to write.

We were having trouble with nose wheel vibration on takeoff, before landing gear retraction. The shaking was so bad it was causing damage to the tail section and nose wheel components. Our hydraulic engineers devised a new shimmy damper for the nose wheel steering that seemed to eliminate the vibration. Both Joe and Walt tested it with positive results.

The Martin company sent down their chief test pilot, Pat Tibbs, to make a test flight. I met him at the gate. Pat was short chunky guy with not much to say, although he did utter something like. "Where is it? I'll make it shake."

I escorted him to the airplane, and as he sat down in the left seat, he exhibited familiarity bred from all the previous certification flights. After the normal pre-flight activities, we taxied to Runway 27R and started the takeoff. As the airspeed increased to flying speed, the nose lifted off, and Pat reduced the power. Holding the airplane just above the runway, in a nose low attitude, so the main gear could not touch the runway, he skidded the airplane to the left, and in a crab, gently touched the nose wheel to the runway. Then he lifted the nose and repeated the maneuver to the right. Side loads caused a sudden and severe shaking of the whole airplane, accompanied by a deafening noise. Instruments were unreadable. The airplane was lurching side to side so violently, Pat and I almost bumped heads. I thought there was not enough runway left to stop. Pat closed the throttles. As the main gear touched, he used full reverse power. With the nose still high in the air, he made the shortest stop possible.

Side stress on the tail assembly caused major damage, and some nuts on the nose gear assembly were only finger -tight. Pat later died in an aircraft accident. Know your limitations.

We made another modification which cured the problem. Later, while I was instructing, the nose wheel torque link broke on takeoff, and produced the same violent vibration and damage. As the airplane came to a stop half way down the runway, two crash vehicles came into view. We had never alerted the crash crew. The noise brought them out.

We lost only one 404 out of a fleet of 40. Landing at Charlotte, N.C.. The captain made an atrocious approach and unusually hard landing. The airplane flipped over, landing upside down. Only one causality occurred. The captain testified that the ailerons locked. No investigation was directed to this probability, because of the appalling approach the Captain had made.

I had previously ferried 404s that had been grounded because the log book revealed locked ailerons. While assigned to engineering, it was discovered that if the adjustable stops on the aileron quadrant became out of limits, hard over aileron demands would cause locked ailerons. The stops had rubber bumpers on the ends. Too much yoke pressure, and a rapid bounce occurred, shutting off pressure. It was also discovered, relaxing yoke pressure would gain control. This information also never reached interested parties.

After the wreckage was shipped to Miami, I opened the belly compartment to look at the quadrant, hoping to check the stops. The whole system had been removed. No one knew where it was.

I know systems on newer airplanes are different and some of the above may not be pertinent, but I hope it will stir the inquisitive.

I had a 1945 Luscombe used to teach the kids. On the second flight, after landing, the left landing gear strut broke. The aircraft swerved somewhat as it settled. Damage was minimal. The bad part, I didn't have a license to fly single engine. Although, I flew single engine in the Air Corps, it was never added to the license. At that time, I was an FAA designee issuing licenses. The Carswell incident was still being investigated. Lots of hot water.

To have single engine privilege added to my license, a check ride was required. The check was scheduled in my Mooney at Homestead General airport. The FAA designee refused to give the check because I didn't have the required training. I went next door and had an instructor write the necessary entries in my log book. The designee must have known the entries were fraudulent. I gave him $25 and completed the ride. So much for regulations. On the ride, the designee asked me to do a chandell. So long since doing aerobatics, I had forgotten what a chandell was. I did a sloppy immelann. The designee exclaimed, "That was no chandell. I didn't know this airplane would do that.!!" So much for memory.

CHAPTER FIVE
AIRLINE SERVICE

Pleasure of airline passengers flying today cannot be compared with yesteryears. When I went to work with Eastern Airlines in 1940 as a cleaner, unions were not important, and the Captain was King. My salary was $95 per month, no matter how much overtime was piled up. Overtime was voluntary. Relations with the company were so good, when the boss said, "I need three men to work overtime", he would get six volunteers. Of course, the 25% unemployment rate in Dade County, made a difference. With the advent of unions, relations deteriorated somewhat.

After I resigned to join the Air Corps, Captain Eddie Rickenbacker sent me a present on each of my birthdays, even in war zones. After the war I returned to my old job in the commissary. The company gave me a bonus just as if I had never left. In case you forgot, Rickenbacker was a World War One ace, a recipient of the Congressional Medal of Honor.

Passenger service was a dream. We didn't have a Public Relations Department. One was not needed. Every employee was a salesman. Today employees are no longer dedicated. Passengers wore coats and ties, and crew meals were a welcome delight. One of our Constellation flights, Miami to Atlanta to Chicago was called the champaign flight. A famous caterer was chosen in each city. Superb meals were served out of each city, on china, with all the champaign you wanted.

When I was working in the commissary, a passenger requested a hot potato be served out of Jacksonville. The DC-3 flight originated in Miami, where meals were boarded. There was no way our equipment would keep a potato hot that long. I sent a teletype to Jacksonville, to have a hot baked potato boarded. Another passenger wanted us to prepare her baby's formula. She didn't know the ingredients. I was instructed to call her doctor. Dedicated employees are missing. Enjoy you peanuts.

A Captain delayed a flight at the terminal because there were no seat covers on the leather cockpit seats. I rushed to the terminal with a set of covers. The airplane had been setting in the sun for some time. In those days there was no air condition. As I rushed through the cabin full of perspiring passengers, there were no complaints. The Captain informed me, "Those leather seats make my pants shinny." Delay a flight today, for this kind of flimsy reason, and see what happens.

After my retirement the fuel crisis was in full swing. The Airline Transportation Association (ATA) designed a fuel conservation program aimed at air traffic control. This was just before the air traffic controllers' strike, the one which resulted in the firing by President Reagan of many controllers. Eastern's part was to provide someone to present the program to air traffic controllers. They gave me the title, "Fuel Specialist". I when back to work at $15 an hour, plus expenses.

I was given a video, made by ATA, explaining ways controllers could help us save fuel. But what ATA really wanted was an improved relationship between controllers and the airlines. A controller with a favorite airline can be an asset, by selectively expediting departures and arrivals. Some of the controllers in the MIA tower were my friends. Many times I received preferential treatment on both training and regular flights.

To chose me for a public relations man seemed nonsensical. Traveling to various airport control towers and air traffic control centers was an education.

The FAA had been hiring personnel under the Fair Employment Act for many years. The results were beginning to show. Before the "Do-gooders" got into the legislative act, air traffic controllers with proper qualifications were chosen from the top of a competitive examination. Now applicants from minority groups are given preferential treatment.

Minorities have only to compete against themselves. Any enterprise that fails to hire the most qualified available individuals is doomed to a deficient operation.

A caste system exists in air traffic control, which separates supervisor from controller. It is more pronounced than the relationship between officer and enlisted man in the Army. It is not a race or sex problem. It is a problem based on something other than ability or efficiency. When a controller is promoted solely because of color or sex, resentment abounds. When a minority controller is kept in a position, even though his performance is borderline, that controller is carried and resented by his fellow workers. Sexual harassment complaints are numerous and lacking justification. – all things that deter efficiency.

Many supervisors believe themselves to be superior to the controllers who work under them. The controllers say the only reason for promotion to supervisor is inability to perform on the boards (actually controlling traffic). This judgment is not without reason. At only one facility did I find a supervisor who occasionally performed the work of a controller to maintain proficiency. At one facility two coffee pots were maintained. One pot for supervisors, and one for controllers. Neither side wanted me to drink from the other side's pot.

About this time in history, a congressional committee toured air traffic control facilities seeking first hand knowledge concerning delays. But to recognize the facts would be political suicide. In reality, in this profession, there is no room for promotions or hiring based on anything other than the ability to do the job better than someone else. In my opinion the air traffic control system, in spite of all the technical advancements, has deteriorated from a once-proud and efficient service organization to just another mediocre government bureaucracy in which individual controllers are no longer recognized for their ability to expedite and control traffic. And today this a contributing factor to the airlines inability to successfully execute on time schedules. The Fair Employment Act required 30% of all new hires be of the minority. Minority is defined as anyone not a white male.

In the past, making schedule was high priority. Pilots reported to operations one hour ahead of departure time. If a pilot caused a delay for any reason, a fine of $25 per minute was levied. The union got rid of the rule. In operations we checked the weather, specified the fuel load, and filled out the flight plan. If we got off late, we cruised at a higher air speed. Today, most airlines do not require an operations check in. Pilots may report directly to the gate. Dispatchers, with a computer flight plan, tell them where they are going, at what altitude, how fast, and how much fuel they are allowed. This a reverse of authority between ground personnel and pilots.

On a flight from Miami to St. Thomas, the flight was oversold. A Marine Chief Petty Officer approached me at the loading gate. His son was in the hospital in St. Thomas, and since he could not board, he asked to ride the jump-seat. I let him ride. You think any Captain would do that today?

Eastern was shutdown because the flight engineers were on strike. We had one Connie which had been converted to haul freight. Only six seats remained for passengers. I was to fly it to Boston with an aircraft engine as the only freight. On arrival at the airport, the airplane was parked at the new 20th street terminal. The gates were all empty. Our part of the terminal was vacant and the hangars across the way were quite. At the airplane was a foreman from maintenance to get me started. Also a family of five, mother, father and three kids stood on the tarmac. They were employee pass riders from Boston. They had been sleeping in the terminal for two days, broke, exhausted, and with no way to get home. The father begged me for a ride. My orders explicitly excluded pass riders. I told them to wait while I made a phone call. I called several vice presidents with the request that I be allowed to take the pass riders. All requests were answered with an emphatic "NO!"

I couldn't, or wouldn't, leave that family behind. On returning to the airplane, I told the father, "It's OK, but you have to promise me the children will keep their seat belts fastened the entire trip. So, take them to the toilet now." Pass riders were allowed to ride ferry flights at the discretion of the captain. I considered this a ferry flight. We just happened to be hauling an engine. Tears in the mother's eyes may have affected my decision.

Air traffic controllers, most of whom are not pilots, are allowed to ride the jump-seat on regular flights for familiarization purposes (called a FAM trip). It's a good way for them to get to know what it's like in the cockpit, but most have never availed themselves to the opportunity. Since a few captains don't like controllers, for reasons I have never understood, perhaps controllers are concerned for the treatment they might receive. Some Captains, like other misfits, don't like anybody. I always welcomed controllers aboard, and did my best to provide needed information.

My presentation of the fuel saving program consisted of showing the video, and then having a bull session. Listening to complaints and exchanging ideas got to be fun.

Before 30 to 40 controllers at the Miami tower, the head of their union (PATCO) came to the mike and proceeded to jump on me with both feet. Directing his remarks toward me, he said, "Eastern has quite a nerve sending you over here to ask for our cooperation after the way pilots have treated controllers. Right now, Eastern has a lawsuit against two of our people in Charlotte." He was referring to a landing accident in which the company tried to establish blame. Had that been the end of the meeting, it would have been a disaster.

My rebuttal was, "I'm sure all of you are familiar with the recent news stories in the press concerning the ALPA's intention to shut down all air traffic in the US with a one day strike." The purpose of the proposed strike was to bring attention to the plight of the industry. "Let me read part of this letter from ALPA to FAA citing particulars that need attention. There's about a dozen but I'll read just a few: one, air traffic controller's pay, two, air traffic controllers working conditions, three, the dilapidated condition of their equipment, minority hiring practices and so on. If you think the pilots are not on your side, guess again." After adding some thoughts on Pilot-controller relations, I sat down and received a resounding ovation.

In the Jacksonville center, I went to sleep while the video was playing. I guess the controllers thought I was getting old. They have an uncanny sense of sniffing out the truth. The job didn't last long, and I thought was not much of a success.

For a long time, requirement of all new hires at Eastern was on hand observation of tower operation for a certain number of hours. I don't know why it was discontinued.

A news paper report: in her final public remarks two weeks ago, FAA Administrator Marion Blakey cited New York, but she also talked about Chicago's O'Hare International Airport where in 2004, the FAA forced the airlines to reduce the number of takeoffs and landings between 7 a.m. and 8 p.m. to 88 per hour down from a high earlier this decade to 130 or more. As a result, according to the *Post,* delays were reduced by 24.5 percent in 2005.

In controller vernacular, peak hour traffic is the highest number of takeoffs and landings in one hour, over a 24 hour period. In 1980, Miami International reported peak hour traffic as 121, 1981/109, 1982/109, 1983/108, 1984/108. . Today you would expect an airport like Chicago's O'hare to have a count much higher, especially with more controllers, all the new runways, taxi ways, ground radar, etcetera.

New airliners don't go as fast as old ones. At Eastern, cruise speed was mach .84. Mach .78 is today's average. Max cruise speed of the B-720 was M . 86. Today's A-320 has a max cruise speed of M .82. Vertical separation was 2000 feet and now has been reduced to 1000 feet. This should almost double in-route airspace. Yet, we hear screams about the crowded sky. True, there are more airplanes in the sky today, but not that many more. Total takeoffs and landings at most major airports today are only slightly more than 1965. New technology and space should handle more than the increase. Environmentalist, in their concern for noise pollution, have caused airlines to practically shut down night flying. Let the airlines return to night flying, and congestion would be relieved. Airlines might even start to make a profit.

On time departures and arrivals, during my 40 years, Eastern's were more than 95%. Arrival and departure delays are defined differently today than in my time. The older definitions were much more strictly measured.

A year passed, the controller strike was over, and the company called again. They wanted me to crank up the fuel saving program again. But, this time it was a pretense to get me into FAA facilities for another purpose. Three months prior, the company began to encounter in-route traffic delays that, it projected for a year, would amount to a loss of 62 million dollars. My job was to find the reason for the delays.

My first stop was the Miami Air Traffic Control Center, where I met Mr. Carter, the chief, and Mr. Cook, his assistant. This was the same Mr. Carter who gained fame (sic) for being the first person to successfully sue a tobacco company for causing lung cancer. My questions were centered around, "What programs or procedures have been changed recently."

As I was being escorted around the facility, I had many questions about a program that the controllers appropriately called "Snitch." This was a computer system designed to help separate traffic, covering the entire US. It had been placed in operation three months previously. When aircraft are too close together, or are on a course that would bring them too close, computers scanning aircraft positions activates a warning. A bell and flashing red light alerts the whole room – I call it a room, but it's more like a huge dungeon with a bunch of not so well dressed people sitting around watching their own personal television screens. When the alert goes off, controllers not busy, gather behind the station that has had the "deal" (let two airplanes get too close together). The Chief insisted, the new program did not slow traffic.

I asked my escort, "What happens to the controller when the Snitch alert goes off?" I was told, "The controller is immediately relieved of duty. A hearing is held to establish the facts and the controller is given remedial training."

Asking to be left alone, I spent the rest of the day talking to controllers on the floor. Here is what I learned. Before Snitch, standard separation was five miles. Now, in order to avoid disciplinary action, separation increased to ten miles, with some controllers, 15 to 20 miles. It didn't take a brain surgeon to figure out that airplanes in trail were stretched out like an accordion, causing delays. That's one reason it now takes longer to fly from Miami to New York than it did in 1965. Also, why major airports can now handle less traffic in a one hour period than in the past.

All commercial aircraft today have the collision avoidance system (TCAS). With this system it would be near impossible for a controller to run two airplanes together, even if he tried. Inaugurating this system should have allowed aircraft separation to be reduced. Yet, FAA mandates more horizontal separation. With en route vertical separation reduced to 1000', capacity almost double. Yet, you still hear about the crowded sky, late departures and delays. It isn't space—it's people who make the rules.

After the Jacksonville controllers were encouraged not to attend my meetings. I saw no use in continuing the program, and resigned.

As I write this congress is again holding more hearings to find out why the airlines have so many delays and lost bags. Someone should enlighten them to the facts. There is no such thing as a lost bag. All missing bags are sitting in a room someplace waiting to be claimed, or they were stolen. Many new airports have been built. Existing airports have added new runways and taxiways. Peak hour traffic is not as high as in the past. En route vertical separation has been reduced, but that didn't help either. Other separation policies has added to the dilemma. All of this after TCAS (traffic collision avoidance system) was inaugurated. Add the fact that airplanes don't fly as fast, people don't work as hard, you should not expect to get there on time.

I read about flights sitting on the tarmac for ten hours while passengers suffer. With overflowing toilets, stale air and hunger adding to the kayos, Captains should declare an emergency. In the old days, when the Captain was really in charge, this would never happen. No real emergency was necessary. We were empowered to take care of passengers, actually charged with the responsibility. I remember one long delay on the ground at DCA. The Captain escorted passengers to the restaurant, and paid for their meals. So much for Captain's authority.

Not all problems are in the air. Ground problems add to the deficient operation. Here is an article from a British newspaper, 2008.

'On Thursday British Airways canceled almost 70 flights after a day of delays caused by baggage handling problems. On what was supposed to be the first full day of operations at Terminal Five, many flights took off with their holds empty, carrying passengers with just cabin baggage.

Some passengers slept overnight inside the steel-and-glass terminal, - reviving precisely those images of delay and decline in British aviation that British Airways said it would banish with the opening of the new terminal.

As a result, Mr. Walsh said, some 36 short-haul flights out of Terminal Five —— mainly short-haul and domestic —— were canceled in advance Friday to ease pressure on staff dealing with unfamiliar procedures and systems. You know what happened with the opening of Dallas and Denver airports.

CHAPTER SIX
A LITTLE HISTORY

A little history to exhibit the progress we have made. If progress of the next 50 years matches the last 50, let your imagination run wild. But, don't forget, everything tends to reaches a plateau. So it will be with aviation. When the SST first went into service, projection was that all of our senior pilots would be flying the SST before retirement. Only a few were built. In a few years they were gone. Economics is, and will continue to be the governing factor.

Communication technology has improved tremendously, but humor has not. My son, Steve, an air traffic controller in the Jacksonville air route traffic control center, working the French supersonic jet liner, asked the flight, "Is it true that the SST grows in length while in flight?"

The pilot answered with the standard explanation, "At high speed, due to the heat from friction, the aircraft becomes nine inches longer." From an unknown source came an immediate response, "Gee, I wish mine would grow nine inches when I get hot." For the next ten minutes most everyone on the frequency had something to add.

That is not the only way to stretch an airplane. During the war, we sent a C-47 back to the States. Douglas wanted to measure the impact of towing gliders. The airplane had been stretched six inches. If something don't stretch, it will break.

In high school, when the air races were held, it was a good excuse to skip school. Not that I was interested in flying. I was afraid to fly. The air races were not like the air shows of today. The airplanes were not as dependable as modern aircraft. Low level races around pylons were visible from the viewing stands. I remember in 1937 two of the racers crashed within sight of the stands. The most interesting event was the "Bat Man." A man dressed in a canvas suit jumped out of an airplane at great height, trailing a wispy plume from a sack of white flour. The canvas attached to his arms and legs allowed him to sail like a bird. His attempts at aerobatics were usually unsuccessful. Even though he had a parachute, he sometimes crashed and killed himself. But the next year there was always someone to take his place. And there was the "Human Glider", William Kuhn, who at the end of a 100-foot rope attached to a Stinson, ran behind the airplane until gaining enough speed to soar like a glider. I don't think he lived very long either.

I marveled at these men with so much courage. But, the urge to fly never materialized, nor did the fear disappear. No one could have been as ill prepared for a career in the air as this author. Somewhere along the line, fear of flying disappeared. Anyone can learn to fly. If you read on, I will prove it.

Early in my career, at airports where there was no low frequency ranges, some captains used commercial radio stations to make instrument approaches. We simply tuned our radio automatic direction finder (ADF), to the right frequency, and the needle would point to the station transmitter. These were approved approaches. Knowing the location of the transmitter, it was possible to make an ADF approach. In order to more positively identify the station, we called the company and asked what song was playing, or what program was on that station. Musical talent lacking, I could never identify the song. As a Cadet, learning to fly, in a Stearman, we had to make approaches and landings with no airspeed indicator. At proper speed, a C note was generated by wing guide wires. Too slow and the note went down the scale. Too fast and the note became higher. The instructor was always hollering at me to listen. I suppose this was the accepted way, a long, long time ago.

After World War Two the airline industry expanded dramatically. Never before had the industry had such a pool of experienced pilots to draw from. Now the enemy would be the nature of the job itself.

During the time that we flew prop airplanes, it was more dangerous to be an airline pilot than to be a policeman. The New York Police Department and the Air Line Pilots Association had about the same number of members. More ALPA members were killed in aircraft accidents than New York policemen were killed in the line of duty over any given period.

During my tenure with EAL, we had a total of 57 highjackings. Most were to Cuba. Only one resulted in a death. A copilot was shot while in-flight.

Bomb threats were more numerous. While on approach to Albany, New York in a DC-8, a bomb threat was directed to my flight. The telephone threat came from a subdivision outside Chicago. The caller was reported to have a German accent. I parked the aircraft some distance away from the terminal, and a thorough search was made by a trained crew, observed by my flight engineer.

After the search was completed, I asked my engineer, "Did anyone look in the cabin compressors inlets?" No one had. Four cabin compressors are located in the nose, just below the radar, assessable from the ground without aid. Those compressors turn at 35 thousand RPM, which would add tremendously to any explosion.

No sooner in climb configuration out of Albany, another bomb threat was received. When a pilot receives a bomb threat, all pertinent information is given. This latest threat came from the same location as the first, and from the same person. A decision to continue the flight was made only after consulting with the whole crew.

I instructed one of the flight attendants to talk with all male passengers. If any had a German accent, I was to be notified. One male passenger fit the bill. He was rather scrawny, dressed in shorts and short sleeve shirt – no place to hide a weapon. I invited him to the galley for a chat. His home was in the same subdivision as the caller. In the course of the conservation, he announced, "I think I know who made the call." This, I thought to be an excellent lead to the perpetrator.

I notified the company to have law enforcement meet the airplane on landing at Ft. Lauderdale. On deplaning, two FBI agents were waiting at the foot of the stairs. I briefed the agents, and asked to be notified of the outcome. The company nor myself were ever contacted.   ,

After the war I had no desire to fly anymore. After a few months boring work in the commissary, my perspective changed. My interview for a pilot position with Captain Jack Lambie, the same Lambie, who with Dick Merrill, made the first commercial nonstop crossing of the Atlantic, went well. He said, "You are just what we are looking for. We will call you in about a week for the next pilot class." Of course, Rickenbacker's order (give preference in hiring to all previous employees who had learned to fly in service), gave me an inside track.

After two months of waiting, I went to Lambie's office to see why I had not been called. He said they could not locate me. My phone number was written on my application, which was on his desk with a note attached, "Working in the commissary." Lambie was a company man. Maybe he wanted to keep me in the commissary department. Two classes of pilots had gotten ahead of me on the seniority list. Seniority lists governed everything, where you were based, promotions, pay and vacations. You can suffer from the mistakes of others. I should have been more persistent.

I was notified on Friday to be in class Monday. That morning I had a wisdom tooth pulled and didn't make class until noon. I was spitting blood in a burp cup for the next two days while my civilian flying career was getting under way.

Ground school didn't amount to much. I think all of the pilots were from some branch of service and lucky to be alive. We did learn that copilots were not supposed to know anything, and that the captain was king. Copilots were not allowed to attend most ALPA (Airline Pilots Association) meetings, even though they were members in good standing. When allowed to attend and vote, their vote counted for only one half vote.

Some time later, when three captains were in a conversation about airplane systems, I joined in. Captain Mel Thayer advised me that, "This conversation is for captains only," and that "I have forgotten more about flying than you know."

"That's probably true," I replied, "And what you have forgotten will not help you one bit." I walked away.

Mel was one of the few weird ones. The only captain who made the copilot keep a written record of everything. Every radio transmission and clearance had to be logged. He kept the papers in his garage until there was no room for the car. He scared hell out of me with every landing. He always came in too fast. One day landing at Boston -- I wasn't with him -- his excess speed caused a collision with a snow bank. The Constellation was demolished, and a fire erupted. As Mel tried to exit through the cockpit side window, he became stuck in the frame, all 250 pounds. The copilot, with both feet on his rump, was able to push him through. He was so cautious, he was dangerous. Flying en route, when given a clearance to descend visually, he would make a 360-degree turn before descending. This was not only unnecessary, it was dangerous and fowled up the traffic behind.

Pay was notoriously low, $165 per month to start. After five years as copilot, I still made less money than the taxi drive who drove us to the hotel on layovers. Expenses were limited to six dollars for every 24 hours away from home. No hotel rooms or transportation were provided. Hotel rooms were five dollars, which left us with one dollar for transportation and meals. During one of the worst snow storms in New York history I was stuck in the old Paramount Hotel, or maybe it was the Edison, from Christmas day until New Years day with no money. There were no such things as credit cards, and my checking account balance was zero. My rich friends came in handy. In New York, from LaGurdia airport, in the middle of the night, to save money, we rode the subway to the hotel. I would not like to do this in these times.

On layovers in Newark, we stayed at a large wooden hotel owned by a famous black preacher. It was a dump with no fire escapes. Afraid of a fire, we purchased escape ropes and secured them next to the windows. On rare occasions, when rooms were scarce, I had to sleep in the same bed with a fat captain. Had this necessity continued for very long, my flying career would have ended, and I would have been back working in the commissary. I remember eating one Christmas dinner alone in Newark at an outdoor hotdog stand near the airport. It wasn't even a good hot dog. Working on holidays, being away from home and family, was an inconvenience that came with the profession. That was one reason for being an instructor, more time at home.

The large number of service pilots hired after the war, with their vast flying experience, and ability to accept responsibility, were to be the moving force that changed ALPA and company attitude toward copilots. Our fleet of airplanes ("Great Silver Fleet") consisted of DC-3s. DC-2s were about gone. So in ground school we studied the airplane, which I was already well familiar with, practiced receiving Morse code, spent time in the Link Trainer, and concentrated on low frequency radio range navigation. All phases of the training came easy. Airlines will always prefer service pilots.

The Link trainer, forerunner of the modern simulators, was a closed stationary box, a mechanical contrivance with a few flight instruments that tried to duplicate an airplane cockpit. Eastern received the first, and maybe the only one with engine controls. It now rests in the Weemes Aviation Museum at the Tamiami Airport in Miami, Florida.

There are no low frequency ranges in existence in the United States today, possible the entire world. In the early days, it was our primary means of navigation. In the winter time a trip from Miami to New York, with many stops, might be conducted without ever seeing the ground, except during takeoffs and landings. Cold fronts sometimes lay on a line from off shore Canada to the Florida Keys. Right on course.

All the larger cities had a low frequency range with four legs. The directional radio transmitter sent out simultaneously an oral Morse code signal, an A dit-da (./-) in one direction, and a N da/dit (-/.) in another direction. So if you were in an "A" quadrant, a strong "dit/da" would be heard through earphones. Speakers were not yet on the scene.

As you approach a leg, the dit/da would gradually change to a steady hum. On the leg, das and dits overlay each other, producing the steady hum. Crossing the leg, the steady hum changes to da-dit. The range is made up of four quadrants and four legs that produce the steady hum. Direction of the legs is permanently set at installation. All legs converge on the transmitter. Going toward the station, volume increases, and going away it decreases. Volume control monitoring was continuos.

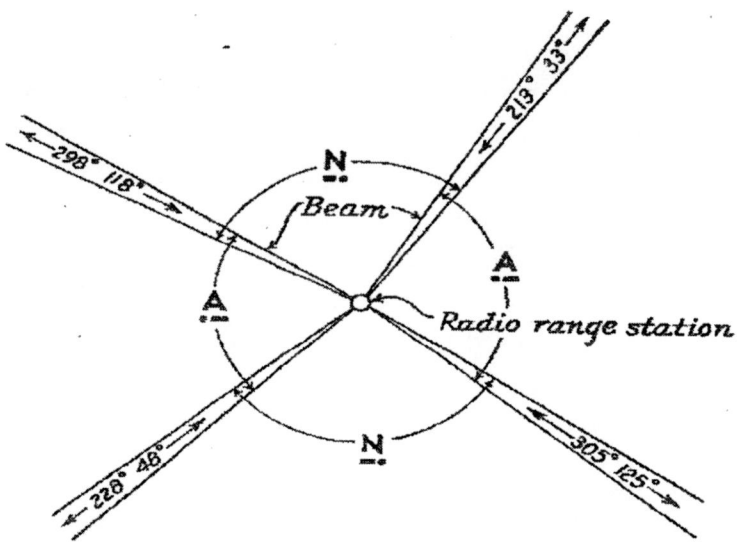

When the ranges are far apart, the legs become so wide as to be useless. The N quadrant is always the north quadrant. If you get lost, a simple exercise will ascertain which quadrant you are in. Cross a leg at a 90 degree angle, convert time to distance, multiply by a factor (I have forgotten), and you have the distance to the station. The area directly over the station is called the cone of silence, an upside-down vertical cone shape that is devoid of sound. At least one of the legs was aligned down the center of an airway like the center line on a highway. We always flew on the right side, if skillful enough. No wonder I don't hear so well.

When making an instrument approach, the cone of silence is a positive location of your position, and usually is the final approach fix. Although, sometimes, fan markers were used. Major airports had one leg that served as the final approach. Minimums were usually 400' ceiling and one mile visibility. Although, not many Captains accepted the restriction.

We lost one DC-3 in the Piedmont area while making a low frequency range approach. Even though tuned properly, the radio was receiving signals from another transmitter far away. Under certain conditions low frequency radio waves are bounced off the ionosphere and received far from their intended destination.

My earliest experience with the low frequency range came soon after graduating from Cadets. Flying a C-47, with only 20 hours as pilot in the plane, and a total flying time of less than 200 hours, I got lost on a cross country flight from South Bend, Indiana to the old Detroit City Airport. The weather was extremely dismal, low visibility in snow storms. Having lived in Miami all my life, that was my first sight of a snow flake. They looked as big as your hand. I thought it serenely peaceful to fly through the white crystalline flakes until they started sticking to the windshield, and the engines got rough.

The simple orientation exercise just would not work, because the range used for the approach was located in Canada. No one had bothered to tell, that in Canada the N quadrant is not the north quadrant. Or maybe I was asleep that day. A few hitchhiking passengers were in the rear. One was a resident of Detroit. He came to the cockpit, and leaning over my shoulder, peering out the side window, he was able to identify a landmark. At a very low altitude he guided me to the airport. The visibility was so restricted, I didn't see the water tank located right on the airport. If I wasn't lucky, I would not be writing this.

When the ILS first came into being, I thought it to be the greatest thing since white bread. The simple display was two and half inch round instrument with two cross bars. One bar, the glide slope, was hinged at the left. The localizer bar was hinged at the top. All you had to do on approach was keep the bars crossed in the center. Weather minimums were 200' ceiling and ½ mile. Visibility was determined by a controller on the ground. He simply looked out the window and identified objects on the ground. Each object was a predetermined distance from his position. A far cry form today's technology. We used the ILS system during the latter part of World War Two. There were no minimum weather conditions. It was possible, in a C-47, to make a blind landing.

During World War Two, overseas, there were no weather minimums. In the Troop Carrier Path Finder Group, we used a better method of making approaches and landings. I think they called it, 'Eureka Rebecca Radar'. It was designed to guide us to drop zones. The system involved a transmitter on the end of the runway. In the cockpit, the receiver was a scope similar to your radar scope. On the scope a vertical line, with range marks, represented longitudinal axis of the airplane. The only blip on the screen was your airplane. So, you always knew your position in relation to the end of the runway. All you had to do, maneuver the airplane to the final approach on the invisible extended center line of the runway. Keep the blip on the scope on the center line. If your heading matched the runway, you were on final. Use the radio altimeter for decent. The radio altimeter was sensitive enough to read height of waves over water. If visibility was less than 60 meters, no one said anything if you didn't make it. Visibility in England was reported in meters. I have seen it as low as 30 meters.

In England there were so many airports, you couldn't fly for 30 miles in any direction without seeing one. With so many low time pilots, night flying and landings were a problem. We were not allowed to use landing lights. Most of the troop carrier air fields were ringed with a circle of dim shielded lights that led you to the final approach. The lights were not visible from directly overhead. They were only visible when in the traffic pattern. And then, only visible from one light to the next. When flying from one light to the next, the string curved as if you were flying a landing pattern. As you turned to final approach, a steeper turn was required. When lined up on final, a funnel of dim lights appeared. Just stay in the funnel. About 500 feet, the glide slope indicator with three lights appeared—white for high, red for low and green for the correct slope. At about 200 feet, shielded runway lights came into view. This system saved many lost pilots during total blackouts.

One night, lost over England, during total blackout, I searched for one of these fields. Unable to find one, I turned on the landing lights. At a very low altitude, what appeared to be a blacked out runway flashed by underneath. I made a procedure turn, and came back ready to land. Just before touchdown, I realized it was a highway – I went looking for another airport.

I wasn't the only one to get lost while using the low frequency range for navigation. One of Eastern's flights, southbound from Newark, NJ. to Washington, D.C., on top of a solid overcast, encountered strong headwinds. Lost and unable to orient themselves, the pilots requested help from Newark operations. Over the radio, the chief pilot gave orientation instructions to the crew for hours. The orientation method just wouldn't work. Finally, the crew spotted a hole in the overcast and spiraled down underneath the clouds. A landing was made at the first airport sighted. The airport was located many miles <u>north</u> of Newark. They had probably reduced speed to conserve fuel and the headwind velocity was greater than the speed of the airplane. They were flying backwards. Crossing the range station backward completely nullified any orientation procedure. Winds aloft forecast were not the best.

Before being assigned a number on the seniority list, each pilot had to satisfactorily complete a check ride. Bill Byers and I were to demonstrate our skills for Check Captain M.A.C. Johnson. Bill, an ex B-24 pilot had never flown the DC-3. My experience made me look good.

After the ride, Captain Johnson gave us each a sealed document containing our grades, to be delivered to the Civil Aeronautic Administration. The CAA would later become the Federal Aviation Administration (FAA). We were not supposed to look inside, but I cheated and took a peek. The CAA refused acceptance. "We don't accept perfect scores on any test," was their reason. I waited another two weeks for one of their agents to schedule a flight check. Two more classes of new pilots got on the seniority list ahead of me. You will find seniority very important.

When the check flight was finally scheduled, there was no available airplane. A scheduled flight was delayed while the passengers sat in the terminal, and we did our bit. Ready to go, the CAA inspector wouldn't give the test in an empty airplane. Another delay ensued while the airplane was loaded with sand bags. And then the check ride didn't amount to a hill of beans. A takeoff and landing. Any fool could see I knew how to fly that airplane. A far cry from today's simulator checks.

Later Captain Mac showed me how to fly the airplane without any flight instruments. He had a piece of heavy brown paper that covered the entire instrument panel and another that covered his side of the windshield. The paper over the instrument panel had only two holes in it. One that exposed the ADF needle, and one for the manifold pressure gauges. Using the ADF needle for heading and the manifold pressure gauges for altitude, he was able to make a half-ass approach. The ADF needle, with some reasoning, will indicate a turn. Manifold pressure will indicate altitude change. When changing altitude, one throttle should remain untouched for altitude reference.

For nine years I gained copilot experience on the DC-3/4/6/7/ 8, Constellations, Martin 404 and B-707/720. Much of this time was spent in engineering, flying test hops. By the time the Convair 440 arrived, I was a captain. Promotions are based on seniority only.

All of these experiences would have been unproductive, had I not remembered.

CHAPTER SEVEN
MORE ON JETS

B-707/720/727, DC-8, A-300

The company wanted me to check out on the B-720. The B-707 and B-720, four engine jets, are so much alike that qualification on either suffices for both. The B-720 was the faster than any commercial jet produced today. When first put into service, we cruised at M.86 (86% of the speed of sound). To conserve fuel, we later reduced normal cruise to M.84. Cruise speed of airliners today is usually less than M.80.

After another ground school, which I didn't feel the need of, the company scheduled my oral examination. Never had I felt so good about taking an oral before. My knowledge of the airplane was extensive, at least as complete as that of the DC-8. I had been instructing on the DC-8 for some time.

Mr. Cope, the FAA inspector, was waiting in his office when I arrived. He had a reputation for being unreasonable on the subject of performance, and had failed some EAL pilots. The examination wasn't going well at all. Although every question had been answered correctly, he seemed to be dissatisfied. On a question about the high altitude buffet chart, which had already been answered correctly, he said, "We are one hour into the oral and still in performance. If you persist in your answer, I will have to fail you."

The buffet chart is an informational chart display of altitude, weight and speed which alerts the pilot to the possibility of a high or low speed stall. A stall is defined as when the wings no longer create enough lift to support the weight of the airplane (usually caused by slow airspeed or increased weight - G-loads, ect.). If you go too fast or experience excessive G loads at high altitude, a high speed stall may be encountered. The high speed stall is caused by boundary layer separation (air moving across the top of the wing is moving so fast, it no longer clings to the surface). Like if you could stick your finger in a glass of water and pull it out so fast it would not be wet.

Although the approach to the two stalls feel the same, they are caused by a different phenomena. Stall warning systems don't warn of a high speed stall. Buffet is the shaking that occurs in both, just before the stall. Go too fast or too slow at a high altitude, or hit a bump, and you get the buffet. Unstable air causes the bumps, which effectively increase or decrease aircraft weight. The high speed stall is a required demonstration on check out. On the DC-8, I made the demonstration at high altitude and heavy weight simply by asking the student to make a 30-degree bank. As the airplane began to shake, I'd ask, "Is that high or low speed stall?" No one could tell. I'd say, "If you pull back and it gets worse, it's low speed. Push forward and it gets worse, it's high speed." Which was not a precise explanation. In the absence of stall warning, you should suspect high speed. The buffet chart was everyday stuff. I had been teaching it for years, and had consultations with the people who put it together.

I am not proud of what happened next. I lost my cool. Uttering a few cuss words, including "Bullshit," I let him know of my exasperation. The remainder of the exam lasted less than ten minutes. Normal time for an oral was two to three hours. He wasn't about to fail me now.

On returning to the training office, still mad as hell, I told Rudy Seymore, my boss, of what had happened, and dictated a letter to Rudy's secretary to be sent to the FAA official in charge of this area. The letter contained a declaration of my belief that Mr. Cope had been failing applicants for giving the correct answer. After Cope received a copy of the letter he called me to minimize his deficiencies and deny the allegations. Everyone at Eastern knew I was on solid ground. But, again my reputation in FAA circles was not enhanced. This is not the best way to take an oral.

Most pilots bent over backward trying to be nice to FAA inspectors because of their tremendous potential effect on professional careers. Bill Byers told me, "I wouldn't be in your shoes for nothing. Suppose you get him for the flight check"

For the check ride, scheduled to go before daylight, guess who showed up for the FAA--Mr. Cope. Monty Chumbley was the check airman. Monty was an old timer. He had something to do with flying Howard Huges' big flying boat, "Spruce Goose".

The weather was terrible with thunderstorms in all quadrants, and a tornado reported in North Miami. In those days thunderstorms were not the deterrent they are today. Weather like that would close any airport today. With lightning all over the place, on the end of the runway cleared for takeoff, I had forgotten the location of the windshield wiper switch. To hide my ignorance, I ordered Monty to, "Turn on the wipers." To pass a rating ride, it is necessary to exhibit command posture. I have often said, "Give me a movie actor who is not a pilot, but can follow the script, and I'll get him half way through the ride before anyone realizes he is not a pilot." I once saw a movie in which Charlton Heston was landing a B-707 in extremely bad weather. He did everything exactly as a professional would do. Inspectors like to see a pilot exercise command. If you don't know the answer, find someone that does.

The weather was so bad, we had to go all the way to Jacksonville to get the landings. After the flight, in the debriefing, Mr. Cope found nothing good to say. He criticized my first takeoff, saying, "Your airspeed on climb out was 20 knots too high."

Reminding him of the weather, I said, "Yes, and if you had not been along it would have been plus 40." Another expression I wish not made. Monty said it was as good a ride as he had ever witnessed. Pilots possess adeptness in various levels, as do FAA inspectors.

After that I instructed on both the four-engine jets, switching from one to the other, sometimes on a daily basis. I always thought a pilot should be restricted to only one airplane, for obvious reasons.

We still didn't have any approved simulators, so all the maneuvers had to be performed in the aircraft. The emergency descent maneuver required a descent from 35,000 feet to 14,000 in three minutes. The procedure gave pilots problems, and cost the company lots of money in repeated training. I suggested they practice the procedure in a chair at home. The procedure had to be accomplished in order; don the oxygen mast without removing glasses (within three seconds), while making an announcement (using the oxygen mast mike button--if you could find it) of your intentions, close all throttles, configure the aircraft, and call for the check list.

Configuration for each airplane for an emergency descent was different. The Boeing configuration was with the landing gear down, spoilers deployed, and no reverse thrust. For the DC-8, reverse thrust was use with the landing gear up.

If the landing gear is extended on the DC-8 at high speed, the doors will be blown off. If reverse thrust is used on the Boeing at high speed, the engines may come off. I lived in fear of forgetting which airplane we were in, and using the wrong configuration. Maintaining proficiency on multiple aircraft is difficult if not impossible.

Training flight engineers on the B-720, I took my son Steve, still in high school, along as copilot. Of course he did all the flying. He exhibited proper use of the yaw damper without my instruction. Where he got the information, I don't know. Maybe from overhearing talk at home. At that time we did not have full time yaw dampers. Don't leave your work at the office.

Before acting as instructor, I flew the B-727 for four hours to familiarize myself. That's when I discovered the stall warning system gives no warning above 10,000 feet. Oh, it will work, but long after the fact.

Early B-727s had an angle of attack indicator on the instrument panel. The sensor was mounted outside on the fuselage just below the captain's window. The system was removed after we learned that the airplane stall is related to other things, not exclusively to the wing angle of attack. Some aeronautical schools today still teach inaccurate information – stall is related to wing angle of attack only.

All swept wing aircraft are subjected to dutch rolls. When the aircraft is not aligned directly with oncoming air, one wing is effectively swept forward, and the other is swept back in relation of oncoming air. Forward sweep increases lift. Sweep back loses lift. Forward sweep increases drag, while sweep back decreases drag. To demonstrate, in stabilized flight kick a little left rudder. The airplane will yaw to the left. The right wing will be swept forward, increasing lift, as the left wing is swept back, decreasing lift. You start a roll to the left. Without inputs, increased drag on the right wing will cause a reversal of forces and cause a roll in the opposite direction. Without corrective action, or a yaw damper, the airplane will oscillate with increasing magnitude. The "Dutch Roll" is capable of destroying the airplane. Recovery training from dutch rolls was a problem with early swept wing aircraft.

B-727 dutch rolls was more critical at higher altitudes. B-707 and 720 were more critical at lower altitudes. Why, I don't know. Captain John Paine was on final approach at Boston in a B-720. When the yaw damper was turned off, dutch rolls took over. His only words were, "There goes the SOB." He was behind the curve all the way to touchdown. John was the company joker, always ready with witticism. One morning after a long night flight, setting in the cockpit, John said, "See that man over there?" A man was propping a small airplane. "He doesn't know a prop from a potfur." Of course, I had to ask, "What's a potfur?" His answer, "To piss in. You dumb ####." Good therapy for an exhausted pilot.

All swept-wing aircraft are required to have an operative electronic yaw damper, one for each rudder. The B-727 was our first airplane to utilize full-time dampers. On earlier jets the yaw damper could not be used during takeoffs and landings. The system simply senses a horizontal slip or skid, and moves the rudder to keep the tail behind the front end. Auto pilots have no rudder channel.

In flight training, I had some trouble with dutch roll recovery at high altitudes, so I practiced until proficient. I was concerned with controlling the airplane without hydraulic flight controls. At 35,000 feet, without hydraulic ailerons, I almost lost the airplane in a vicious dutch roll. Then I tried one without hydraulic rudders. The airplane will not dutch roll when rudders are disconnected. There is no way to move the rudders on this airplane without hydraulic pressure. When rudder pressure is shut off, the rudders simply free trail (streamlined behind the fin). That's when I learned that without hydraulic pressure to the rudder, the rudders becomes a mechanical yaw damper. Rigging of control tabs are such, when the surface is moved out of the streamlined position, the tab will move in the same direction, forcing the control surface to move in the opposite direction. Same result as a yaw damper.

Other control surfaces on other airplanes are rigged the same way. You can see this on the ground if you push up on an aileron, and watch the tab go ahead in the same direction, or if wind has displaced a control surface. Some people still believe the control tab always moves opposite to the control surface. Aileron, rudder and elevator tabs are rigged the same way on many airplanes.

In a DC-8, sitting in the cockpit, you can tell where the elevator is by feeling the yoke. The yoke only moves the tab. If the elevator is up, you will not be able to push the yoke forward, without great pressure. The elevator has lead weights in the nose. This is why, on airplanes with gust locks, it is sometimes difficult to engage the gust lock.

The FAA required dutch roll demonstrations in a 30-degree bank until Boeing heard about it, and informed us that this could precipitate the loss of the tail section. I developed a simple method of recovery, cross-control ailerons and rudder. This worked so well that recovery could be made with your eyes closed. For some unknown reason, the method was never adopted.

Two yaw dampers are required for dispatch. Leaving San Juan for Miami, the pre-flight inspection revealed both to be inoperative. Rather than take a big delay, I chose to go on to Miami, After climbing to altitude, I depressurized the rudder and had a fine trip. Had the FAA caught me, I would have been grounded. FARs may have been written by people who may not understand the system.

Eastern operated the B-727 in and out of St. Thomas for many years when the one and only runway was only 4,010 feet long. And sometimes you needed that extra ten feet. All takeoffs and landings were to the east. Night operation was prohibited, as was landing with standing water on the runway, and prevailing wind required all takeoffs and landings to be to the east. Although, I have, under unusual conditions, taken off to the west. Due to the mountains, wind shear was always present on approach, sometimes severe.

Since every landing was a short field landing, I occasionally used reverse thrust before touchdown. When all conditions were right, at the threshold, idle reverse thrust was applied -- this only closes the buckets. After touchdown, with speed brake extended, reverse thrust was applied. I know the manufacturer and operators take a dim view of this. This procedure allowed a stop without using brakes. I didn't try this on a passenger flight until after testing a few times on training flights. Test revealed, on both old and new models good rudder control, even with the nose high in the air and asymmetrical thrust. This is a tip of what not to do, unless your life depends.

We had just received delivery of some new DC-8/63s. With larger engines and other modifications, they were somewhat different from the older models. Qualification is automatic, if you are rated on earlier models. I told my boss that I didn't want to instruct on the new model until I had a chance to fly it myself. In the middle of the night I got a call from someone of authority, "We got a 63 on the ground with an engine out in Charleston, WV. How about deadheading up and flying it back?" I thought the person on the other end of the line to be out of their mind, and gave a resounding NO. The Charleston airport, built on top of a mountain, was not suitable for the smaller DC-8s, much less the 63. To ask someone with my experience to fly it out on three engines was not very smart. Make your own decisions. Don't let someone else set the trap.

The next day I was scheduled to give a proficiency check on the DC-8/63 to two senior captains. This assignment was also refused. I had flown copilot for both the captains and was not about to show my lack of knowledge. They finally let me familiarizes myself before accepting students. Don't bite off more than you can chew.

Training flight engineers, with no rigid flight plan or curriculum, gave me the unique opportunity to play with the biggest toy I ever had. A flight engineer instructor took care of the students. One of my favorite maneuvers was to take the DC-8 to about 20,000 feet, and put in a gentle dive with full power. When the airspeed reached the red line, I would pull up the nose to a 50 or 60-degree climb angle. On reaching about 35,000 feet, with the airspeed rapidly deteriorating, I'd close the throttles, release all back pressure on the yoke and kick in a good amount of rudder. From this almost vertical position, and airspeed below 100 knots, the stall warning system was never activated. It only senses angle of attack. The airplane went weightless in a modified wing over. The feeling of weightlessness is exhilarating. Also, I think, it has a calming effect. There is nothing calming about the recovery. The airplane falls like a rock, almost straight down. Without over stressing the airplane, it takes at least 25,000 feet to get level again. I had to stop doing that maneuver when my flight engineer complained. I don't blame him.

These maneuvers were always accomplished in controlled airspace with radar following.

Another way of killing time was to start at high altitude, and attempt to make an approach and landing without using any flight controls. This I had practiced many times. After learning the effect of landing gear and flap extension, I was able to maneuver to the final approach using throttles only for control. I could hit the airport, but never made an actual landing because the airplane was never exactly over the runway at the proper speed. Inboard engines are more effective for pitch control. Outboards are better for turning. Buzzing deer in the Everglades was also fun, but not too smart. In retrospect, I should have not been doing these things. On the other hand, I learned much.

If lucky enough to be doing air work at sunset, I'd make the sun come up in the west. With the sun half way below the horizon, at a high altitude, I'd make a rapid dive until the sun completely disappeared. Then with full power, and a maxim climb, I'd watch the sun climb right out of the west. Enjoy your simulator.

Air traffic around MIA was getting so congested, EAL worked a deal with the Bahamian government to use the airport at Freeport, on Grand Bahama Island, for training. At Eastern's expense, an ILS was installed.

The only runway was not too long. Each student had to make at least one no-flap landing. Minium landing speed was 200 knots (same speed as the shuttle uses for landing). Tires were rated for 210 knots. Yes, there were lots of blown tires. It didn't take long to change requirements. Touch and go landings replaced the full stop requirement.

The Mary Carter Paint Corporation lodged a law suite against Eastern. They claimed our training airplanes were making so much noise, it was reducing value of a subdivision they were building just west of the Freeport airport. The no flap landing did require a lower than normal approach.

During the trial, I traveled to Nassau to testify. This was when England still maintained dominion over the Bahamas. It was a sight to see the

Judge and attorneys wearing white wigs. The case was settled with an injunction against Eastern to cease training at Freeport.

I don't know just how the politics worked. There was communication between Eastern's officials, Washington and England. Within a few days, the injunction was rescinded. We were back in business.

One of the many stupid things I did occurred at Freeport. In a DC-8, with only one copilot and one flight engineer we flew to Freeport. The copilot was new, and had no experience as engineer. He needed landings. The engineer was an old timer; who had qualified under the new contract with only three landings. After giving the copilot some landings, it was time to go home. I decided to let the engineer fly back. I told them to change seats. The copilot advised me that he did not know how to operate the panel. I said, "That's alright, I'll tell you what to do."

On the flight back to Miami, it was worse than flying solo. The engineer, in the copilots seat, had trouble keeping the airplane on course. Between giving instructions to both, talking to the company and ATC, it was more than I could handle. Profit from mistakes of others.

Dade County decided to build a new Training Jet port (TNT). Much political and media debate had been kicked around as to the best location. The environmental voice was loud. People were concerned the noise might disturb the alligators. A test conceived to determine the noise level alligators would endure, required installation of sound measuring equipment out in the swamps, down in the saw grass. The test would require a DC-8 to fly real low over the instrumented area. Bill Byers did the flying and the test proved nothing. The decibels recorded were so low, they wouldn't bother me, much less an alligator. I don't know if it was faulty equipment or the saw-grass insulation. Sound from wind blowing saw grass was loud.

The environmentalist wouldn't let us fly over alligator country below 6000 feet. Once, with one engine inoperative, and needing to get down to landing weight, I dumped 50,000 pounds of jet fuel over downtown Miami at 1500 feet. Which was perfectly legal. Sometimes we get our priorities mixed up.

TNT was still in the planning stage. Dave Vaughter, a captain from New York, came down for a checkout on the DC-8. I had taken Dave through the simulator training. Our first flight period would be flown for the benefit of a television camera crew. Station WTVJ was making a documentary pertaining to the proposed airport. Politics was rampant.

One camera on a tripod was bolted to the floor in the companionway just behind the pilots. We flew around while they rolled the cameras, taking pictures of the purposed site in the everglades. We couldn't spend four hours taking pictures of the swamps, so I asked, "What would you guys like to see?"

They wanted to see some landings. With Dave at the controls, his first landing at Miami was a hard one, a three bouncer. The television crew told me that they would call and let me know when the program would be aired. The call never came.

A couple of months later at home, I was taking a shower and heard a commotion in the living room. My wife and kids were laughing and hollering for me to come see TV. A 30-minute documentary on the proposed airport was being aired. Shots taken from just behind the pilots of Dave's hard landing was the background for the titles. Since the camera was rigidly attached to the airframe, as the airplane contacted the runway, tremendous vibration of the picture occurred. As we became airborne again, the picture smoothed out. You could hear me saying, "Let her down easy!" Nevertheless, when we hit the ground again and the same scenario was repeated. My son, laughing, said, "Boy! What an advertisement for Eastern!" That was the first time I realized the back of my head was bald.

The first month Dave flew the line in a DC-8, he made the cover of LIFE magazine, but not for his tennis. On the cover was a color photograph of a DC-8 in flight, gloriously in flame. One of the engines was on fire and the flame reached almost to the tail. The normal check list and fire extinguishing procedures didn't dowse the fire. It didn't go out until the fuel supply was shut off at the tank. The shut-off valves in the pylon were notorious for not completely closing. This knowledge was gained when the airplane was new from test and training flights. When shutting down an engine, we used the engine fire shutoff lever, which shuts off everything. Sometimes the engine continued to run at low RPM. Since this lever shutoff oil, we could have ruined an engine. So much for lack of knowledge. Dave knew to shut off the fuel at the tank, and probably saved lots of people.

The

EAL FLIGHT 63 APRIL 8, 1967

The DC-8 had large fuel selector levers located on the flight engineer's panel, one for each engine. Positions were marked to allow selection of various tanks. At the very bottom of the selector was the off position. Somewhere along the way I learned the perplexity of the valves and the system. The "Off" mark shut the fuel off completely. When the lever was moved ever so slightly, toward the up position, the internal valve flipped open to an auxiliary tank, without the handle moving. To the naked eye, the fuel to that engine was shut off, but the engine was actually receiving fuel from the auxiliary tank. Once on a training flight, while my flight engineer instructor was in the rear, I placed all the fuel selectors in this apparent off position. When he returned to the cockpit and spied all the fuel selectors in the off position and engines still running, he was dumbfounded. If you think this was stupid, I agree.

Bob Valentine was an FAA inspector. While he was giving a flight engineer a rating ride, and while the student was in the rear, I demonstrated and explained the fuel valve perplexity, i.e., running an engine with the selector in the apparent off position.

After landing, while taxiing toward the ramp, I suggested to Bob, "Why don't you show the student how to run an engine with the fuel selector off?" This was a setup. I had run the auxiliary tank dry. Bob liked to demonstrate his knowledge. So when he performed the demonstration, he simply shut off one of my engines. I liked to humble FAA agents in the air as much as they liked to screw me up on the ground. Not a smart thing to do.

On another flight with Bob, taking off on 27R at Miami, giving a captain rating ride, I was in the right seat. The first takeoff was planned to be normal, but right at lift off, the number four engine fire warning bell sounded and the red identifying light came on. After silencing the bell, I announced, "This is no drill. Just fly the airplane straight out, and I will handle it."

If anything will set off panic in a pilot, it's an in-flight fire. Having performed the engine fire act hundreds of times in training, I did not hesitate to shut down the engine, and discharge the extinguishing agent without the use of a checklist. The fire indications disappeared momentarily, then came right back on. I asked Bob to go back in the cabin and visually check the engine.

We had only two shots at putting the fire out and I didn't want to waste the last one. Bob came back and said, "It's still smoking." So I discharged the last bottle. This time, it had no effect on the indications. Then I asked Bob to take another look. He reported this time, "It's really smoking now!"

I decided to get the airplane on the ground right now, and advised the tower we would be landing on 27R with an indication of an engine fire. FAA procedures are — were; that if you report an in-flight fire, controllers had to advise Washington immediately, and everybody has to write letters. Whereas, an indication of a fire requires no special reports, but is handled by the crash crew in the same manner as if it were an actual fire.

Up until this time no check lists had been called for nor accomplished. I suspected the FAA would take a dim view of this. While on approach, my engineer asked, "Clyde, do you want any check lists?" I answered, "No. Just do what needs to be done." I made a high speed, power off approach and touched down smoothly. When the aircraft stopped on the runway, the crash crew made a visual inspection of the engine, and communicated no fire or damage. I taxied to the hangar.

If the DC-9 Value Jet that crashed in the Everglades had used this rapid method of getting on the ground, the passengers may have had a chance. But if they had, the pilots would have been in a heap of trouble, writing letters for the next six months. Running the check list for cockpit smoke removal can take up to nine minutes. They could have been on the ground at Opa Locka in two minutes.

After deplaning, Bob and I walked over to the engine. By now maintenance had the cowling removed, and there was no evidence of a fire. I asked Bob if the smoke he saw might have been the extinguishing agent seeping out. "Oh No!" he said, "That stuff goes WHOOF, right through the engine." I told him, "You would fail a student if he told you that on an oral examination. That stuff is trapped in the accessory section. Otherwise, it would do no good." He had erroneously identified the extinguishing agent leaking out as smoke.

The cause of the fire warning was a hot bleed-air leak that caused no damage. Bleed-air leaks were by far the most common cause of fire warnings on jet engines. I didn't have to write any letters, because Bob knew that I'd done the right thing. Non use of checklists was never mentioned. I suggested to the training department that students be advised of the possibility of misidentification of the agent, but the information was never processed. By now I was conditioned to accept denial. Another one of my mistakes, not persistence.

When the new training airport in the everglades (TNT) opened, the tower was manned by controllers from Tamiami Airport who had to drive 40 miles to, and 40 miles from work. Instructors refused to use the airport because no crash equipment was available there. After a week, with company assurance that crash equipment was in place, I landed there at 6AM with a locked brake.

On the landing rollout, the tower transmitted, "Your left landing gear is on fire." I turned off at the end of the runway, stopped, jumped out of my seat, and opened the front door to see the gear. The fire had gone out. Although still smoking, it didn't look bad. Realizing we had no way of getting down from the airplane, and to be safe, I told the pilot to call for the crash crew. Fifteen minutes later a tractor-like vehicle arrived. We climbed down a ladder extended from the makeshift fire vehicle, and rode over to the tower.

After notifying the company of the incident, the tower chief, who was a friend of mine, took me to breakfast at a small Indian restaurant on the Tamiami Trail. I asked him why the arrival of the crash crew was delayed. He explained, "We don't have a crash crew. We have to depend on volunteers to drive the truck. The first guy I asked to drive the truck said, I'm not going out there! That airplane is going to burn up!" Also the vehicle used, without rubber tires, was not allowed on the paved areas, due to damage that might occur to the surface. The driver turned out to be the grounds caretaker. Besides the caretaker and my crew there was a total of four people on the entire airport in the Everglades.

I notified the company there would be no more training, at least by me, at TNT until acceptable crash equipment was in place. Over night, an old rubber-tired vehicle was driven down from Ft. Lauderdale, and we were back in business. If someone don't look after safety, no one will. Now that's a brilliant statement.

Eastern had to send mechanics and equipment from Miami to change the tires, replace brake assemblies, and to start the engines. Another half-day wasted. To start a jet engine, great amounts of compressed air is required. Someone suggested that we needed an air tank stationed on the airport. In those days some commercial jets did not have the capability of starting the first engine. Some airports, without maintenance facilities, kept an air tank for starting engines.

To make a few extra dollars, I tried to locate one. I found one at Freeport in the Bahamas. The tank, a large one on wheels, with it's own air compressor, was available. I planned to buy it, move it to TNT and charge for usage. FAA approval was needed. Stupid government regulations prohibited any maintenance equipment on the airport. So the whole idea fell through. Throughout our use of the facility, any of the older jets that shutdown all engines had to wait for a start unit to be driven from Miami. Government regulations are not always befitting, but always hard to change. Politicians don't necessarily know anything about aviation.

We lost a DC-9 at TNT. Shooting night landings, it crashed in the swamp a hundred yards south of the runway. The airplane was demolished. The crew received only minor injuries. No crash crew ever responded. Even a day later, the crash vehicle was unable to reach the scene. Some hunters supplied swamp buggies to reach the wreck.

The crew, battered and shaken, walked in the dark, out of the swamp, across the runway, and climbed the stairs up to the tower cab. The captain knocked on the door. When it opened a surprised controller asked, "What are you all doing here?" The captain replied, "We came to report an accident." Since that was the first inkling the controllers had of an accident on their airport, it was quite an embarrassment. Noise of the crash was not heard inside the air-conditioned cab. It's not unusual for a training flight, when shooting landings, to be given carte blanche clearance for takeoffs and landings, especially if he is the only one in the pattern.

Today TNT sits useless. Rarely do any airplanes use the facility. The airport is uncontrolled (no tower facilities). Only one government employee, not a controller, is on duty at any given time. What a waste of money.

Two army officers from Brazil, Colonel Abicair and Major Santos, arrived to get a rating on the B-720. I have forgotten their titles, but between the two, they were in charge of just about all flying in Brazil. The Colonel spoke some English, the Major almost none. I never understood why the students were given to me instead of Monty Chumbley. Monty spoke fluent Portuguese, while I had trouble with English.

At our first meeting, since I spoke no Portuguese, I declared that all communication had to be in English. The Major responded with jabbering like I'd never heard before. The only word I understood was "English." Colonel Abicair translated for me. "Don't worry, we both speak English." To teach with hand signals would be a chore.

Instead of the Brazilians, Monty was assigned a pilot from some Bahamas airline to train on the DC-8. On the rating ride, taking off on 27R with a simulated engine failure, the student jumped on the wrong rudder. The airplane went off the airport so low over 36th street, it caused a panic in one of the hamburger joints. Patrons ran for the exit. The control tower thought it was an accident and hit the panic button, which sent the crash crew. Monty said it was one of his most hair-raising experiences.

Monty told this story himself. Taking off on a regular passenger flight, he mistakenly took off without a takeoff clearance. Just as they broke ground, the copilot said, "You know, we weren't cleared for takeoff." Monty had mistaken received a clearance meant for another airplane. The copilot was new, but that was no excuse. Don't be afraid to open your mouth in the cockpit, even if you are new. Due to Monty's popularity, no violations were forthcoming.

I gave the Brazilians their simulator training. In the airplane, on the Majors first takeoff, climbing out with a big grin on his face, he uttered the same phrase over and over. When asked, the Colonel translated --"Look at me. I do it, first time! Look at me. I do it, first time!" He wasn't flying the airplane. He was just hanging on. I often wondered what happened to those guys.

Before the use of all the new technology pilots were required to know the systems of the airplane in detail. A favorite question of some FAA agents giving an oral examination on a jet was, "Trace a drop of fuel from the fueling hose through every component until it exits the engine exhaust." If you can do this, you have fairly good knowledge of the fuel system. Airline pilots today are not required to display detailed knowledge of systems. But if you take the time to learn, you will be a better pilot.

The first A-300 fatal crash was flown by their chief test pilot. This time, there was no argument about pilot error. At an air show in France, he made a fly-by using auto flight and was unable to disconnect. Then, there is the story about the A-300 in a holding pattern near Kennedy. They were unable to turn off the autopilot. Not until lengthy communications with ground personnel solved the problem (crew didn't know how to operate the autopilot), were they able to land. They could have run out of fuel.

Here is a synopsis of an A-300 accident------

PROBABLE CAUSE: "The probable cause of this accident was the inability of the pilot flying to assess properly the situational condition of the aircraft immediately upon touch down with No. 1 engine reverse inoperative, thereby causing an adverse flight condition of extreme differential power application during the landing roll resulting in runway excursion and finally an overshoot. Contributory to this accident is the apparent lack of technical systems knowledge and lack of appreciation of the disastrous effects of misinterpreting provisions and requirements of a Minimum Equipment List (MEL). Sources: »» Aircraft Accident Report / Air Transportation Office (ATO)

I once had a student on the M-404,, who on the first day of training said, "Clyde, if the FAA is not going to ask the question, I don't want to hear about it." My answer was to the effect; I have only one program – teach you everything I know about this airplane. The more you know about an airplane, the more confidence you will have. Confidence to handle any emergency is a must for a good pilot. He later to became chief pilot, and I overheard him give the same advice to a new hire. That was good.

Many aircraft have vortex generators on the exterior surface of the wings and stabilizers. Vortex generators are small (three or four-inch) airfoils attached to a surface, which protrude almost perpendicular into the air stream. Their purpose is to redirect airflow to conform to the surface, thus delaying separation. They are all attached entirely with glue.

One of the greatest technological advancements of our time is the making of glue. When I was a child, my mother mixed flour and water to form a paste for gluing pictures on a poster. Now glue is sued in assembling many aircraft parts. The B-727 contains 300 pounds of glue. But don't worry, it is waterproof. I don't know how this information could help a pilot, unless it is just the fact that every item of knowledge acquired makes learning the next thing just a little bit easier.

Today pilots are taught, not how a system works, or to rely on memory, but to use the checklist and manual in the cockpit. This saves money in the training process but doesn't take care of unforeseen emergencies.

Some pilots, when checking out on a new airplane, have trouble with the walk around. Usually, the day of the flight check, you and the FAA inspector will arrive at the airplane early, to provide extra time. The inspector will lead you around the airplane asking questions. You are expected to identify every visible gadget. Expect to be asked to open all hatches that are accessible. You better know what is inside.

My method of teaching was to identify everything the first day. Thereafter, never simply point something out and identify it. For instance, open a wheel well, point to a an accessory, and ask the student to identify. If he can't, don't give the answer. Ask more questions, such as; What does it look like? Is it electrical, hydraulic, manual ? Is it connected with wires or pipes? What's it connected to? Usually, he will come up with the correct answer, and never forget.

Another airline lost a DC-8 in a night crash caused by lack of training or inadequate training. The flight lost one communication radio. The remaining radio had to be switched back and forth from the air traffic control frequency to the company frequency. Approaching the airport, when the landing gear was extended, an unsafe warning appeared for the right main landing gear.

A missed approach was executed. Only one communication radio was available. Conforming to company procedures, a call was made to the company for instructions on how to handle the situation. With only one radio it was necessary to change frequency. Now instructions from air traffic control could not be heard. With the controller screaming instructions and warnings, which of course could not be heard because the crew was talking to the company on the one and only radio, the airplane flew into a mountain.

The DC-8 has a button on top of the wing, one for each main gear. The button pops up when the main gear is down and locked. The button is mechanically actuated. It is plainly visible from the cabin. This indication is much more reliable than electrical indications in the cockpit. I wonder if those pilots were, on their walk around, required to identify the pop up button. A little better training and thought about procedures would have allowed a lot of people to live a little longer.

Weight and balance was a weak subject for most pilots. They didn't generally understand the delicate balance required for flight. The limitation section of all airplane manuals displays the most forward and most rearward permissible location of the center of gravity (CG). These points are defined as a percentage of the mean aerodynamic cord of the wing. The airplane must be loaded so the balance point will fall within these limits. FAA examiners usually ask applicants to quote the center of gravity limitations. Unfortunately, reciting a few numbers doesn't connote understanding.

To demonstrate the importance of these limitations, I would balance a yard stick (36 inches long) with my finger near the 18-inch mark and ask, "Assume this stick is the length of the airplane. Take a guess as to how many inches tolerance there is between the forward and rear limits of the center of gravity." Student answers were varied and inaccurate. The answer is about two inches either way. If the center of gravity is not within these limits, it is not legal to takeoff. Performance goes out the window.

If the airplane is loaded so the center of gravity is near the aft limit, it will go faster. I once made an in-flight test on a Constellation, transferring 2500 pounds from the front of the cabin to the rear, and gained 15 knots airspeed with no added power or loss of altitude. The reason for the increased performance with an aft CG is that in such instances the horizontal stabilizer on the tail is not required to carry as much negative lift, thus decreasing drag. When Eastern learned this, they deliberately loaded near the aft limit. Pilots complained and loading practices did an about-face. Get the CG too far aft and it's like riding on top of two greased ball bearings. Vertical control is touchy. All certification performance speeds are derived with the CG at the most forward allowed position.

If the airplane inadvertently pitches nose up, which has happened on freighters when cargo slides toward the tail on takeoff, forward pressure on the yoke by the pilot produces an aerodynamic force on the horizontal stabilizer in the opposite direction of that needed to recover. If enough forward pressure is applied to the yoke, the stabilizer trim motor is not powerful enough to move the stabilizer toward the airplane nose-down position. Manual trim is also useless. No one is strong enough to overcome the leverage.

When this phenomena was discovered on the B-727, a suggestion to install a more powerful motor was made. But, it never happened. It wouldn't matter anyway, if the motor had a clutch. A clutch is required to prevent the motor from burning up.

I wonder if lack of this knowledge could have been a contributing factor in the Fine Air DC-8 accident in Miami. The airplane pitched up sharply on takeoff, stalled, and crashed just off the airport boundary, killing everyone in the plane and some on the ground. Cause was determined to be cargo not properly secured. It slid aft. Stabilizer control could have been regained simply by relaxing forward pressure on the yoke. NTSB report never mentioned this. When training pilots in the Flying Tiger simulator, this maneuver (cargo sliding aft) was always included in the curriculum. On the check ride, if it happened before V1, and you didn't abort, you failed.

I was giving an oral to two FAA inspectors. One of the inspectors had represented the FAA in an accident investigation in which a four engine jet (Convair-880) crashed on the Atlanta airport. So I asked him some questions about the cause. He exhibited lack of knowledge of minimum control speed on the ground. The accident occurred on takeoff of a training flight. A severe cross wind existed. When an engine failure was simulated, the crew lost control on the ground, and all were killed.

Federal Air Regulations (SR422B) demand that an airplane, experiencing a failure of the most critical engine at the most crucial point during takeoff roll will still be able to stop on the remaining runway, or able make a safe climb out. The most critical engine is always one of the outboards. While still on the ground, it is determined by the crosswind. In flight, either outboard is the most critical.

All swept-wing aircraft, while still on the ground during takeoff in a crosswind, tend to weathervane downwind, whereas all straight wing airplanes tend to weathervane into the wind. With the advent of swept wing aircraft, this information was not readily available. Most instructors, to help the student, will fail what they think is the least critical outboard engine. In this accident the most critical engine had been failed, and the crosswind was severe enough to cause loss of control. I posed the question, "How is the most critical engine determined, while still on the ground?" Neither knew the answer. When I explained the method, both refused to accept the explanation until I produced a letter from Boeing confirming my explanation. I tried not to embarrass them. Sometimes, pertinent information never reaches the pilots who need it the most. An instructor should never emphasize his knowledge to a student. Don't be a know it all. But, don't let pertinent information stay obscured.

Two young newly-hired pilots arrived to check out on the DC-8. Both were small, slim and not very muscular. We met at night at the passenger terminal and used an airplane that had just arrived on a regular flight. Both seemed to be overwhelmed in the dark cockpit of such a big airplane. Both had trouble making a normal turn. They seemed to be doing the right things but were not strong enough to do a good job. I shut off the hydraulic flight controls and asked one to make a turn. No matter how hard he tried, the airplane stayed almost straight and level. After changing seats, the other pilot couldn't make a decent turn either. I said, "If you guys had a hydraulic failure, you would set some kind of record for distance in straight and level flight".

The flight was canceled. I suggested they join a health club or start working with weights so we could try again in a couple of weeks. Both came back somewhat bulked up and completed the training. Strength alone is reason enough to prefer male pilots over female. I suppose today strength is not needed. The computer does everything.

Colonel Frank Borman, the former astronaut, was our new leader. His guidelines for hiring new pilots may not have been the best. I know he was wrong when he got rid of all the maintenance foremen who did not have a college degree. Quality of maintenance clearly declined after that.

We hade a student from the Ivory Coast (Cote d'ivoire) who needed a rating. Other instructors have given up on him. EAL had an open-end contract with the US State Department to provide the training, both ground and flight, to Bakery (pronounced 'Backery') Soconoko, necessary to acquire a rating on the DC-8. Time or money was not a consideration.

Bakery, a son of a high ranking official in the Ivory Coast government in Africa, was to return to that country, and head up a department equivalent to our FAA. Bill gave me Bakery's records, and I could see I had another problem. The student had 45 hours in the simulator and 45 hours in the airplane. A note exemplified his status: "Has yet to make an unassisted landing." This was unheard of. Most pilots check out with a maximum of ten hours in the simulator and ten hours in the airplane.

There was a joke around the training department, that I could teach a chimpanzee to fly. I had actually talked to a Hollywood animal trainer about the possibility. I had visions, after retirement, of building a model airplane and teaching a chimp to fly. The trainer told me, not to get a chimpanzee, get a monkey. He said a chimp would learn. But, he would fly away and not come back. A monkey would learn from rote. What a blow to the piloting profession that would have been.

Talking with two of Backery's instructors, I learned one of the reasons they quit flying with him was his bad body odor. The odor in the cockpit was unbearable. They were right. I say this with no disrespect. I liked Bakery and we got along fine.

Bakery was the worst pilot I ever flew with, and this would be akin to teaching a monkey. After the first flight, in the debriefing, I brought to his attention the fact of his bad body odor. Bakery's understanding of

English was not the best. Sometimes I had to resort to hand signals to ensure comprehension. The only time I was sure of his perception, was when he broke a big grin and said, "YAh! YAh!" Using hand motions while talking, I told him of his bad body odor by holding my nose and pointing under my arm. Then pointing at him and saying, "PHEW." He gave me the big grin and the "Yah!" No way did I berate him. I did suggest deodorant spray cans.

The next day as I entered the scheduling office, Jack Wright, the scheduler, asked, "Did you SMELL Bakery?" From then on the cockpit smelled like a two-bit house of ill repute.

For the next two weeks I flew with Bakery almost every day. One of his problems, failure to control the airplane on landing, had to be corrected. On landing, if the airplane bounced or was headed off the runway, he just sat frozen, refusing to make the necessary corrections. After explaining his problem many times, I too was about to give up. I used my method of dragging the runway many times. It helped some.

Before giving up, I decided to give it one last try. While flying from the right seat, I explained, "Bakery, this is your last chance. You are going to land this airplane this time if it kills me. What ever happens, I won't help you. If you crash and we burn up, I'm dead." I removed my earphones and slid my seat to the extreme aft position. Then I turned my back to Bakery. In that position there was no way I could reach the controls. I could see the engineer. He was worried. This was at TNT, the training airport, and we were the only traffic. Just before crossing the threshold on final approach, without Bakery's awareness, I positioned my seat so I could reach the controls if necessary. Bakery, sweating like a pig, bounced the landing, added power and maintained control straight down the runway. This was the beginning of what little improvement that I saw. My act must have been convincing because the engineer complained to my boss.

Giving Backery an engine our landing, we had simulated the failure of the #4 engine, and were on downwind leg with no power on #4. The # 3 start lever vibrated to the off position, shutting down that engine for real. This occurrence happened often on the early model DC-8s but rarely on the later models. No one in the cockpit, other than I, noticed it. I watched intently as the airplane, with two starboard engines out, veered to the right and slowly descended 500 feet. I wanted the student to recover himself. A picture is worth a thousand words. Bakery, not realizing what had happened, did nothing but turn the yoke to the left as far as it would go, which deflected the spoilers and almost stalled the airplane. I suppose he would have crashed in the swamp had I not taken the controls and brought in the two engines.

On his rating ride every maneuver was borderline. I would have given him a pink slip. After the last landing, I told Bakery to turn off at the end, and set the brakes. I knew that Frank Harrell, the FAA inspector sitting on the jump seat, was on the fence as to passing or failing. I had worked with Frank before and observed his flying, which was not too impressive. I took the 'bull by the horns', slapped Bakery on the back, shook his hand and congratulated him for passing the ride. Frank, surprised that I would try to influence his decision, threw up both hands and exclaimed, "Wait a minute!" The student fails or passes only at the determination of the FAA, but I believe my actions swayed Frank. Bakery got his license. Frank was my tennis partner. So, our relations were better than common.

After Frank wrote out the temporary license and left, I advised Bakery to never fly this airplane again, "You will kill yourself or someone else." Sometimes I was torn between my duty to get the student a license, and my feelings that this guy is in the wrong business. This time I was sure he was in the wrong business. Had he been an Eastern employee, he would have never been approved. My Corner tells me, I probably made another mistake. See, I told you, anyone can learn to be a pilot.

If there is anything racist in this, you are putting it there. We parted friends, and he sent me Xmas cards from Africa for years.

A few months after Bakery left, a CIA agent visited me at home. I was questioned for an hour about Backery. The agent would not tell me the reason for the interview – probably building a psychology profile.

All airplanes have a method of removing rain from the windshield. The DC-8 had the best system. Use of engine bleed air was directed across the windshield. It was so effective, the surface looked dry. The only drawback, it required so much engine bleed air, available power was restricted. It could not be used during takeoff of go around.

CHAPTER EIGHT
TIPS

Effort may be the most qualifying quality that makes a good pilot. We needed 500 new pilots. Applicants were given a test at the University of Miami. Those that failed were weeded out. I was assigned the job of evaluating all new hires. Their experience varied from high time SAC pilots to low time Cub pilots. In an Aero Commander 500, I'd take five at a time and judge their abilities. After a couple months; it dawned on me, I could not predict which would make good airline pilots. Exemplary ability will not help, if you don't show up for work. Years later, I flew with most of these new hires – line flying as well as ratings. Some of the low time cub pilots performed better than the SAC pilots. I believe, effort and memory to be the most important traits.

As copilot, I flew with most all our senior captains. Later, some of the same were my students. I have never witnessed an older pilot that could do as top-flight a job as he did earlier. However, experience always offset the ageing process.

Instructor-student relationship should be congenial and firm from the beginning – it's always easier to loosen the screw, than tighten. I once trained a group of pilots from another airline. They were under undue stress. Their employer had informed them, failure of the course equaled dismissal. The first day of simulator training, one student was half hour late. I told him, "Late again, don't bother coming." Then I informed the class, "I have to turn in a proficiency report on everyone. I promise you, I will not say or write anything about you until you and I have discussed and agreed on the matter." They all successfully completed the course.

If you are a smoker, don't despair. The nicotine might give you an advantage. Federally funded studies have proven nicotine gives pilots an advantage in memory, problem solving and reaction time – the main attributes needed by a pilot. One government sponsored study at Sanford University, tested qualified non-smoking pilots in simulators. Forty pilots were separated into two equal groups. After a given time in the simulator for familiarity, the group was split. One group was pasted with a nicotine patch. The other group received a placebo. For the next week they flew the simulator everyday under these conditions, repeating the same maneuvers. Qualified instructors graded each pilot on each maneuver every day. At the end of a week, the nicotine patch and the placebo were switched without pilots knowledge. Pilots never knew who was wearing the real patch. The test was repeated for another week, exactly as the previous two weeks. Each student was rated and given a grade on each maneuver every day.

Most studies disclose split conclusions. Not this one. Every pilot while wearing a nicotine patch scored higher on every maneuver every day than he did while wearing the placebo. The above test was repeated with another set of pilots. Results were the same. I am inclined to take studies with a grain of salt. But this evidence could not be overlooked. Other world wide studies revealed similar results. An Air Force study concluded, smokers have an advantage over non-smokers in the field of memory, reaction time, and problem solving. Another Air Force study, to find out what happens to a person when they quit smoking, revealed these advantages are lost forever. The British government has suggested, pilots on long flights wear a nicotine patch. Also, doctors are beginning to use nicotine to treat alzheimer disease. So much for a smoke free America. Recent findings indicate that smoking burns fat.

The Office of Aircraft Crashes in Geneva Switzerland records worldwide accidents. Total accidents listed: 16,345----number of people fatally injured: 118,316----accidents with casualties: 41%----accidents without information on casualties: 17%---- number of people injured: 86,768. I don't know the time period.

Causes of accidents were assigned as follows: Human error 68%----Technical failure 20%----Weather 6%----Sabotage 3%.

And here is where they happened: Landing 51.3%----During flight 27.5%----taxiing 05.%.

Other sources may paint a different picture about accidents. Most incidents may occur in cruise flight, simply because more time is spent in cruise. But any pilot should know, takeoff, initial climb, approach and landing are the most hazardous. Basic Flying Rules: try to stay in the middle of the air. Do not go near the edges of it. The edges can be recognized by the appearance of ground, buildings, sea, trees and interstellar space. It is much more difficult to fly there. If you lose an engine in a two engine airplane, you can always reach the crash site. The Piper Cub is the safest airplane in the world; it can just barely kill you.

Seriously, the aborted takeoff, a maneuver required for all ratings, usually comes as a surprise. Early in my career I developed a method of improving safety in all takeoffs. On all of my takeoffs; after takeoff power was established, instead of keeping my hand behind the throttles – an old procedure to prevent throttles from slipping back, I rotated my hand to a position ahead of the throttles. This saved time incase of an aborted takeoff. At my decision to continue the takeoff, I rotated the hand to behind throttles. This also alerted the crew as to which way we were going.

The best part of this procedure is, it makes a pilot think of takeoff conditions before the takeoff begins. V1, the decision speed, is not always the time you may decide to stop or go. On extra long runways, you may have plenty of runway to stop well after passing V1. Conversely, on a short contaminated runway, you may plan a decision speed lower than V1. Rarely will you make a balanced field length takeoff -- stop distance equals available runway. This procedure somewhat eliminates the surprise component. I am sorry to say this method was not widely adopted. I taught my son, when learning to fly small airplanes with retractable gear, leave the gear down so long as there was enough runway ahead to safely stop.

The only time you get to practice the abort is in the simulator. I warn you, in the airplane it is not the same. Simulators are programed according to manufactures specifications. Those people are human too. The profit motive does not disappear. The abort may be caused by a multitude of reasons. Performance wise, power loss is the most critical. The airplane is certified to accelerate to V1 and either stop or go. Stop distance is certified without use of reverse thrust. Runway overrun is used to compute available stop distance. The only thing you can be sure of is, it will come as a surprise.

If you start an abort at exactly V1, from the time you close the throttles and apply brakes, your air, airspeed will increase appreciably. This is due to the laws of momentum (an accelerating object continues to accelerate in relation to opposition forces). If you are accelerating, and stop immediately, everything would break. People writing the regulation were aware of this. A two second delay is built in the equation. If you are a pilot, you know two seconds is not enough. A moving airplane has never been known to stop, or stop accelerating, immediately. The main wreckage of the DC-9 that crashed in the Everglades, went in so deep it was never found.

A DC-8 aborted takeoff in Australia. The aircraft slid off the airport. Someone prepared a computer generated video presentation of the accident. The cockpit voice recorder was synchronized with the video. After takeoff power was applied, there was no talk in the cockpit. Speed was near V1 when the Captain's voice was heard , "Ah shit!". Over engine noise of reverse thrust, as speed decreased, as did remaining runway, another "Ah shit!!". As the aircraft departed the airport, a louder and even more expletive was heard. The voice recorder is supposed to be an aid in accident investigation. This one might have told us more than we wanted to know. The three most common expressions (or famous last words) in aviation are: 'Why is it doing that?, 'Where are we?' And 'Oh S...!'

American Airlines lost a B-727 in a landing accident at St. Thomas with many fatalities. When an airliner comes in for a landing with the airplane configured for such, and suddenly conditions change that prohibit a landing, for whatever reason, the workload in the cockpit is heavy. Although it is easier in a jet than the older prop airplanes, it is a difficult and demanding task that requires reconfiguration of the airplane.

This approach was high and too fast. Touchdown was made farther down the runway than normal. The captain was indecisive about making a go-around. A go-around was started. Wing flaps were raised to the takeoff position. As the airplane accelerated, the takeoff warning horn sounded (confirmed by the cockpit voice recorder). Wing flaps must be in the takeoff range to prevent this warning. A loud intermittent horn is distracting, to say the least, and must have had a bearing on the captains decision to abort the go-around. Trying to stop with not enough runway ahead, the aircraft slid off the airport, across a road and into a gasoline station where it burst into flames. Had the pilots been expecting the takeoff warning, I think it would have made a difference in the outcome.

This accident, I think, was a result of information not being decimated. On the earlier model B-727s, due to a faulty wing flap follow up system, the wing flaps when moving from down to up, did not stop moving where they are supposed to. When moving from full down, up to takeoff position, they stopped just before reaching the takeoff range, thus the warning. Moving from up to down, the system worked fine.

I had previously tested all our B-727s and found 70% of the fleet reacted as described above. It's a simple test. On the ground, extend the flaps to the full position, then raise them to the takeoff position. Advance the throttles and listen for the warning. More information that was never advertised. If we can't learn from the experiences of others, the learning process is severely handicapped. I made a half-hearted attempt to contact American without success. Some of the old models are still flying. It might be a good idea to test all airplanes.

One of our DC-9s, landing at Charlotte, came in too high and fast. With poor braking conditions, he slid off the far end of the runway. I don't remember the damage or fatalities. Reading the NTSB report, the flight data recorder read-out showed a decrease in air speed to 60 knots as the airplane neared the end of the runway. Airspeed increased to 80 knots as it slid off the end. When asked, what caused the increase, investigators claimed the reading was inaccurate at low speed. When I asked the recorder manufacturer to explain the increase in airspeed, I was advised, "The recorder is at least as accurate at low speeds as it is at high speeds. Plus or minus 3 knots."

For years I had a theory about reverse thrust on a jet engine at low airspeeds. If too much reverse power is applied at lower speeds, total thrust is forward, thus explaining the increased speed at Charlotte. Although no one agreed with me, the company made preliminary plans to run a test. It would be a simple test. All you have to do is set the brakes and put full reverse power on the engines. Release the brakes and see which way the craft goes. The engine manufacturer assured us that no harm would be done to the engines. The test never materialized,

I could readily visualize what was going on in the cockpit. With the end of the runway coming up, whoever was flying had those throttles back as far as they would go. Just like any normal pilot would do.

All jet engines have one primary thrust instrument. The EPR (engine pressure ratio) is simply a pressure differential between the front and rear of the engine. The difference between the two is always forward thrust. Reverse thrust is attained by closing buckets on the rear of the engine, causing engine exhaust to be deflected sideways and slightly forward. This produces an overall net rearward force as the deflected air meets the on-coming air. For this reason, reverse thrust is very effective at high airspeeds, and becomes less effective as speed decreases. My theory: At low airspeed and full reverse power, EPRs are doubled, but reverse air resistance is decreased. A net force of forward thrust is achieved.

We know with low power you can backup. Don't try with full power. Before reverse thrust was used to depart the gate, I ran the test and wrote the procedure. On most jets, when backing up, brake application will set you on the tail. Nose wheel steering is oversensitive. Maybe, you learned this as a child – backing up a tricycle.

A British airliner was operated for months with unusually high fuel consumption. The cause was finally discovered. Tiny holes in the fuselage were expelling pressurized air, which gave the same effect as engine reverse air. Air directed sideways produces almost the same resistance as if it were a solid stick.

While I was assigned to the Flying Tiger operation, one of their DC-8s got stuck in the mud at Kennedy. Their tugs were unable to pull it out. One of the foremen told of trying to back it out using reverse thrust. He said, when using full reverse power, it only went in deeper. If anyone ever runs the test, I'd sure like to hear about it. In any case, if you are running out of runway, it is not a good idea to use full reverse power.

Now all training is accomplished in simulators. Pilots are not completely trained to handle all emergencies. Emergencies in the airplane are more distressing than the same emergency in a simulator. I have trained pilots in the simulator to handle a certain emergency and observed their inability to handle the same emergency in the airplane. You cannot program the fear component in the simulator. No one can predict the outcome of this influence on individuals.

Eastern Airlines had a contract with Flying Tiger Airlines to use their airplanes to haul freight. To setup the training program, I needed re-qualification on the DC-8. An FAA inspector, another pilot and myself, traveled to Los Angeles, to use their simulator. Due to programing of the box, neither I nor my companion could do a decent job. The inspector would not even try. It was necessary to learn the indigenous behavior of the simulator before completing the check.

Consider an engine failure on takeoff. You may have practiced the maneuver in the simulator many times. But when it happens in the airplane with hundreds of souls behind, it won't be the same. There is a way to mitigate this problem. Know the procedure and the logic well enough to perform it in your sleep. This, you will have to do on your own. Repeated recall will do the trick. It will, give you the needed confidence. Confidence breeds perfection. Due to reliability of jet engines, you may fly your whole career and never experience an engine failure on takeoff. But it is not worth the gamble.

Should you lose an engine on takeoff, don't expect the same performance attained on certification flights. On certification flights the surprise component was not present. Pilots had practiced the maneuver to perfection. Trimming of the airplane was accomplished with the use of a sophisticated instrument not available to airline pilots. With asymmetrical thrust, and the airplane trimmed so as to center the ball in the turn indicator, maximum performance cannot be obtained. This was determined by in-flight tests. A string, attached to the nose just below the windshield, gave visual picture of air direction. To get the proper trim, keep the ball one ball width out of center. I have forgotten which way.

If you have never experienced hydroplaning on landing, you are in for the thrill of your life. It's like a force pushing from behind. It is caused by a small ridge of water on the surface that builds under the leading edge of the tire and progresses back until the whole tire losses contact with the surface. Many accident have been attributed to this.

On landing gear with dual wheels, there is a way to mitigate hydroplaning. A formula exists that predicts the speed at which hydroplaning will occur. The only variable in the formula is tire pressure. The harder the tire, the lower the speed at which hydroplaning will occur Conversely, the softer the tire, the higher the speed at which hydroplaning will occur – or was the other way around? It doesn't matter. All you have to do is carry asymmetric pressure in paired tries. Example, increase pressure in one, and decrease pressure in the other. A change of 10% reduction and increase will result in a 20% difference in the speed at which each tire will hydroplane. Thus, one tire will exert braking at all times. Why air carriers never adopted this method, I don't know. Tire manufactures said it was OK.

Grooved runways are better than those not grooved. However, they become filled with dirt, rubber and debris. If airport maintenance doesn't keep them clean, they are useless. That's a huge job. Not many airports are diligent.

While bird strikes are not as numerous as in the past, they are still a hazzard to be dwelt with. With the advent of strobe lights, strikes were cut in half. We also learned, landing lights, even in the daytime, improved the rate. We lost an Electra taking off at Boston. The engines ingested a flock of small sea birds. There were no survivors.

Just the other day, US Airways lost an A- 320 from birds. The aircraft, taking off from LaGuardia, ingested birds in both engines. A successful landing was made in the Hudson River. No casualties occurred. The media has made the pilots to appear as superhuman. The pilots were confronted with a situation in which there was no choice. Any good pilot could have accomplished the feat. I wonder if anyone remembered to activate the ditching switch. The ditching switch closes the outflow valve and other vents. Structural failures did not occur due to the smooth surface of the water. Although, one engine did depart the airplane.

When we received out first A-300, I looked into the engine mounts. Pylon mounted engines are suspended by only three bolts. When you see the size, it will alarm you. The aft bolt is a shear bolt. It is designed to shear if engine contacts ground or water. Purpose of the design is to allow the engine to depart up and over the wing. Other airplanes utilize the same method to mount engines. If the engine went under the wing, let your imagination take over. I would like to know if this engine went over or under the wing.

I can't testify to engine certification requirements of today. Older test required: Five, five pound birds be thrown in the intake, all at once, without reducing engine power. The A-300 engines were certified by throwing the birds in one at a time. Common sense tells me, the engine might handle one at a time, but not all at once.

One of the most difficult maneuvers, the emergency decent, presented a memory problem. In the DC8, many students failed this maneuver. It costs lots of money to climb back to 35,000 feet, and repeat the whole maneuver. The FAA required in sequence: Put on the full-face oxygen mask without disturbing eyeglasses, close the throttles, announce to crew with mask mike phone (the transmission switch was well hidden), 'emergency decent'. Then call for the check list. Next, depending on which model you are flying today, reverse thrust on all four engines with max power, or maybe a lesser power on the out boards, or on some models, no reverse on the out boards. Slow to landing gear extension speed, and extend gear. Maintain max gear speed in decent, and start to level 2000 feet above target altitude. All of these actions must be accomplished in sequence. You have three minutes to get from 35,000 feet to 14,000 feet. Descend more than 50 feet below clearance altitude and you will have to repeat the whole maneuver. I encouraged students to practice the maneuver at home. Sitting in a chair, verbally giving commands, and going through the motions, will make the actual test effortless. Here again, don't leave your work in the cockpit.

The B-727 makes an excellent emergency decent. With spoilers fully extended, at max speed, you can come down 18,000 ft. per/minute. Expect a whole lot of shaking.

Landing---If I were you, the auto-land would never get a workout. Every landing adds to experience. Some international Captains make only one landing a month. No one can retain proficiency with this limiting practice. Suppose, a baseball player got to bat only once a month. Same goes for auto-throttles.

Companies encourage the use of auto throttles for fuel efficiency. Veteran pilots know, maintaining a constant airspeed, sometimes requires throttle repositioning, just as your car does when traveling on hilly roads. Contrary to ground pounders beliefs, winds aloft do not always flow on a level plane, like roads in hilly country are not flat. Even in the jet stream, flow is not level. Up flow increases airspeed, while down flow decreases airspeed. Jockeying the throttles will use more fuel than just letting it ride. Driving in the mountains, you wouldn't maintain a constant speed or use cruise control if you wanted to save fuel. Or would you?

Reduced power takeoffs were introduced to conserve fuel and increase engine life. The down side is; this extends the time you are in one of the most critical phases of the flight. Anti noise takeoffs were introduced to please residents around airports. Early on, pilots fought a losing battle, just as with reduced power takeoffs.

Airplane manuals, in the engine limitation section, reflect a maximum EGT and time limit for takeoff. You might find a limit for takeoff of 555 degrees for takeoff, and a time limit of five minutes. For acceleration (takeoff power in flight), temperature limitation is the same. But, time limitation is only two minutes. Why the difference? An engine that has been running at cruise power has higher internal temperatures than one in takeoff position. If you start with higher temperatures, time restrictions are a must.

I still hear pilots talk about when making an instrument approach, at what altitude does transition from instruments to visual occur. Transition should never occur. You hear instrument instructors emphasize scan, and rightly so. When landing, your scan should also be in and out of the cockpit. Even in VFR weather, you should always know at what airspeed touchdown was made. You can't do this if your scan is totally out the window.

Pilots who have both hands on the yoke during takeoff or landing are asking for it. You can't control everything this way. You are not flying. You are just hanging on. If one arm is not strong enough, maybe, you should pump some weights.

A note about the rate of climb indicator. The old instruments measure almost instant vertical speed change. In rough air, fluctuations were so fast, sometimes indications were up, when you were actually going down. With the advent of jets came the Instantaneous Vertical Speed Indicator. It should not be called Instantaneous. The new instrument has, besides a static sense, an inertia sense. Up or down will not register a change until inertia input is in that direction. If you don't believe this, watch the instrument as you rotate. Just after rotation, indication will be down about 300' per minute.

Our jets came with a true mach meter. It had an altitude sense. This did not make it true. Speed of sound is relative to temperature only. It did not have a temperature sense.

I am not familiar with all the new safety features pertaining to a coupled approach and auto land. After certification of coupled approaches on the DC-8, I tested the equipment. While coupled to 9L ILS at Miami, at 500 feet, I activated the on/off switch, rapidly from on-to-off-to-on – to simulate a momentary power failure. The flight director switched from coupled to normal so fast no flags appeared. There was no oral warning. If you did not hear the click of the selector, you would never know. The airplane would go wherever it was last pointed. All ILS facilities have standby power systems. Use is automatic. If power is lost to the main system while you are making a coupled approach, the switch to standby power is so fast, no one would know. This was confirmed by actual test at MIA.

A word on check list. Like the name implies, should be used after the action, not as a work sheet. I encouraged pilots, when they first take a seat, to make a thorough pre-flight cockpit check. Everything that can be seen, touched or felt should be checked. A good way, take an area one at a time (side, floor, overhead, instrument panel), search, secure and test everything in that area, even if it is not on the check list. Then, when the check list is read, you won't have to lift a finger, if you have not missed anything.

When instructing, to save time, I rarely used the check list. But, if a student failed to call for the proper check list at the proper time, there was hell to pay. Quite often, I bet the student a coke he would forget the checklist at least once. The two engine landing was a bitch. It is standard procedure to call for the final checklist at the same time 'gear down' is called. On a two engine landing, gear down is not called for until landing is assured —never above 500'. Once the gear is extended, a go around is impossible. It's too late for a check list. If an instructor accomplished the check list as in line flying, too much time would be wasted. An instructor that needs a checklist is in the wrong business.

Most pilots like to buzz. To observe the terrain sailing by so fast, is stimulating to say the least. It is also a way to get yourself killed. If you have to buzz, be sure to trim the airplane so forward pressure on the stick or yoke is required to maintain level flight. That way, if something unforseen happens, the airplane will go up, not down.

Pilots attitude toward passengers is not the same as it was in my day. Pilots should not be just a cog in the wheel that gets people from one point to another. Passengers pay your salary. It behooves you to have them choose your airline again. On a flight from Miami to Tampa to Atlanta, meals were boarded in Miami to be served to passengers that boarded in Miami. Due to the short leg, the meals would not be served Miami passengers until departure from Tampa. Passengers boarding in Tampa were advised of no meal service before boarding. After takeoff from Tampa, a flight attendant came to the cockpit with news of an irate passenger who had boarded in Tampa. He was shouting, cursing, and generally condemning the company because he had no meal. People seated around him were upset, and the flight attendant didn't know what to do. I told her to take my crew meal and serve him. And be sure to announce in a loud voice, "This is the Caption's meal. He said to give it to you. He said to tell you, he hoped you appreciated it, and that you would fly Eastern again." The result was a batch of derogatory remarks from other passengers directed toward the irate one. This created a bond between passengers and company. As passengers deplaned in Atlanta, many complementary remarks were forthcoming.

On a M-404 flight training, a mile east of Key Largo, all of a sudden there was a Navy jet sitting in tight formation on my right wing. He had his flaps down and dive-brake extended in order to maintain the slow speed. I didn't recognize the interception maneuver, and thought he wanted to play. I descended a few feet and slid under him, coming up on his right wing. He peeled off, and I never saw him again.

On returning to the training office, there was a message for me to call the Commandant of the Naval Base in Key West. I called, but was unable to contact him. That shook my faith in the Navy, to realize no Commandant was available. This was during the Cold War.

In a few days, when contact was finally made, the Commandant informed me that I had been charged with penetration of the International Defense Identification Zone (ADIZ). All papers had already been mailed.

Thirty one days later I received a registered letter from the FAA advising me of the charge and to show cause why my license should not be revoked.

My flight never penetrated the ADIZ. If anyone was lost, it was the Navy pilot. The charge could not be true because I was shooting landings at Miami at the time of the alleged penetration. Needed for exoneration was confirmation from the MIA tower as to where I was at the time of the alleged penetration. Tower radio transmissions were saved on tape, but for only 30 days. Harry Martin, the chief controller said, "Sorry, Clyde, the tapes were erased yesterday." I had the distinct feeling, someone was out to get me.

O.B. Bivins, Director of Training, wrote a nice letter on my behalf, and that was the end of it. I can understand the dilemma experienced by Navy radar controllers, with more than 100 blips on the scope at any given time. Most of the targets would be squawking VFR (as I was), which gave the controller no identification. When two blips merge and separate (happens all the time), it is impossible to determine which one they had been following.

A note on B-727 instrument switching panel. The selector switch for the vertical gyro cannot be switched from normal position to AUX and returned to normal rapidly. If you do this, the system freezes up. You will be left without a flight director on both sides. Switch to aux again, and you are still out of business. It may take more than three minutes for the system to re-boot. Same applies to compass switching. The system requires, when switching from normal to aux, the switch be left in one position for a second or two. I don't know if this was ever fixed. I know simulators were not programed to duplicate aircraft.

My first jet as captain was the Boeing 727. With three tail-mounted engines, this airplane was to be he workhorse of the industry for many years to come. Harry Byrd was the FAA inspector on my rating ride. He tried to trick me with an inappropriate and illegal departure clearance. We had an argument in the cockpit and got off to a bad start. He obviously didn't understand air traffic control regulations. I announced to the crew, "This flight is being taken under protest, and we will settle this when we get back." If you want to make an enemy, this is a good way to start. Personality can sometimes get you in trouble.

The check captain should have intervened, but said nothing. Byrd was overbearing and antagonistic throughout the flight. He tried his best to fail me, but without success. He made me repeat a no-flap approach that I thought was perfect, saying, "You were too low over the outer marker." I repeated the approach, making the same profile, and dared him to flunk me.

After the flight, the check captain still had nothing to say. I reported Byrd's mistakes and attitude to Thad Royal, who was in charge of 727 training. That's when I learned Byrd had been failing some good pilots. During a previous squabble with Harry, Thad got so mad he almost kicked the door down.

I didn't see Harry for many years. Nearing retirement, Flying an easy 727 turnaround, Miami--St. Thomas--St. Croix--Miami , he gave me a line check. He had probably forgotten our spat of earlier years, and screwed up again.

On the approach to St. Thomas, I neglected to switch my flight director to approach mode. It made no difference, since this was a visual approach. After landing, my flight engineer told me. "I tried to bring your attention to the flight director, but Byrd wouldn't let me. Twice I tried to get your attention, but with gestures, he said No." I made a note of the event and asked the crew to do the same, just in case the incident ever came up.

Some time later, as a pilot representative, I was asked by Less Leach, director of training, to attend a disciplinary hearing being held for one of our pilots. The meeting was held in the FAA office at the Miami International Airport. Among the many people present was Harry Byrd.

After the hearing concluded, the high-ranking official presiding over the meeting asked if anyone had anything else they would like to bring up. I had no previous plans to bring anything up, but since I was now officially representing the pilots, I thought it would be a good time to bring up the St Thomas incident. After advising the head man of my desire, he cleared the room, except for himself, the person recording the proceedings, Harry Byrd, myself, and Less Leach.

Now the administrator, looking straight at me, not too respectfully, said, "What is your problem?"

I stood up and read my notes of the St. Thomas episode and added, "I charge this man with interfering with the safe operation of my flight."

Mr. Byrd, sitting across the shinny mahogany table from me, stood up when asked to respond, and gave an account of his long experience with The FAA. He said, "I certified that St. Thomas airport."

I quickly interrupted with, "And that's another mistake you made." During my whole career the St. Thomas airport was rated as a black star airport, one of the most dangerous in the world.

Mr. Byrd was disciplined for his behavior, and didn't show on Eastern property for a long time. My name sunk deeper in mud in FAA circles.

On a wet or slippery runway, it is possible to safely land in a severe crab. Here is one of my experiences. Flying copilot on B-720, we had used so much fuel dodging around the storms that on arrival at SDF we did not have enough fuel either for an alternate airport or delayed landing. A mean looking line of storms was approaching from the west, moving much faster than we had judged. A high speed approach to the south runway put us in extreme turbulence and rain, but visibility was not too bad. The tower reported wind of 30-40 MPH from the southwest. I could see the wind was much stronger at our altitude. A 30-degree crab into the wind was required to stay aligned with the runway. If we didn't land on this approach, the field would be closed. We were trapped with not enough fuel for another attempt, or get to an alternate.

Twice during the approach, Ernie said, "You are too fast! You will never get it stopped." It occurred to me that if we cracked up, it was going to be on the other end of the runway. At about 100 feet, we heard the tower say, "Do not acknowledge, wind 260 at 75." The touchdown was smooth, on the numbers, with lots of extra speed and a crab of not less than 30 degrees. If the runway hadn't been wet, the tires would have ripped right off. We slid somewhat sideways straight down the runway with no problem stopping, even though no brakes were used. Only reverse thrust and rudder was used for directional control and drag. I don't think another Captain would have let me make that landing. Ernie and I had been flying together for some time. And I had more time in the airplane than he did.

The same trip, a week later, we had a problem with the rudder trim control while on the ground in SDF. We thought it not serious, and we continued to Miami. The next day I checked with maintenance to see what they had found. A structural failure was discovered that would have caused a full deflection of the hydraulic rudder if the trim control had been moved to either extreme position. It is a pre-flight check to move the control to both extreme positions. Had this check been made after the failure, the next takeoff would have been made with a full deflection of the rudder, and without the knowledge of the pilots. It is not likely that an accident could have been prevented. Lucky, Lucky.

Having flown the big jets as copilot so long, I had a great deal more experience than many new Captains. For a month I was assigned to fly with a good friend. On his first flight on the B-720, with a check captain on the jump seat, he said, "Clyde, you make the first takeoff, and you handle the gear and flaps." I did all the flying from Miami to Detroit, making stops at Atlanta and Cleveland. The check captain did the necessary paper work, and did not make the return flight. He signed the required papers without ever witnessing a takeoff or landing. Purpose of the check captain for the first 25 hours line flying is to insure competency.

On the return trip, I made the first landing at Cleveland. Leaving Cleveland, the new Captain said, "Im ready now." He made the takeoff. As luck would have it, just after being airborne, the #4 engine stuck in METO power. After the 'ah shit', the Captain said, "Clyde, you better land it." We left the engine running at high power until final approach.

All this might sound like stupidity aloft. In reality it worked out fine. Smart people know when to delegate duties. The Captain flew until retirement, and did an excellent job.

When the company inaugurated 100% simulator training, I negotiated an agreement that required a competent copilot to fly with new captains for a certain number of hours.

Not all Captains exhibited command authority. Taking off at MIA on runway 18 in a stretch Connie, we experienced an engine failure just after takeoff. The Captain asked me to fly the airplane while he talked to the company. I heard him say, "Let me talk to the chief pilot". And then, "What do you want me to do?" This was one of the few that abrogated their authority.

Years later, leaving the Newark terminal in a DC-8, the rudder pedals were locked. The adjusting rod, attached to the bottom of the instrument panel, had fallen down between the pedals and locked the rudders. With a flashlight, I was able to correct the problem. I wrote a letter to Douglas asking for a fix. Douglas answered with assurance the problem would be fixed. The problem was corrected on Eastern's fleet. Other airlines never corrected the problem. Safety systems can always be improved.

CHAPTER NINE
OPERATION AND TRAINING

If you wonder why you don't see any A-300s on the ground at DCA, read this.

The company had just received delivery of the first A-300 (Airbus) and was seeking approval from the FAA and Eastern pilots for operations into Washington National Airport (DCA). Without pilots approval, the plan was doomed. We were the only airline with grandfather rights to fly long flights out of DCA. I was hoping for approval. The ALPA wanted me to check out on the new airplane and the company also wanted me to fly it. With only a couple of years left before retirement, I refused.

The MEC (Master Executive Council) mandated the OAT (Operation Training Committee)–of which I was Chairman, to make an in-depth study of the feasibility of the A-300 operation into DCA.

With no schooling, I flew the airplane once. With Bill Preissner in the right seat, I said, "Bill, just keep these French flight instruments programmed, I don't want to know how anything works." I flew it for an hour, making several takeoffs and landings. It was so easy to fly, I could have passed a rating ride -- all except the oral examination. But, I did comment on the over sensitive rudder. Later, one crashed because of this flaw. After takeoff from Kennedy, according to the NTSB, the copilot overused the rudder in wake turbulence. I could never understand how the airplane passed certification test. Every airplane is required to have a maneuvering speed (VA—the speed at which maximum deflection of any control surface will not over stress the airplane). Their air speed was in that range. Structural failure caused the accident.

On board an A-300 ferry flight to DCA (Washington National Airport) with a member of my committee, Mr. Borman and some of his staff were also on board. We were going to demonstrate the performance and noise level of the new aircraft. Bill Preissner was the captain of the flight.

I liked Borman. He was once considered by the Republican Party as a candidate for President, which I was all for. But he was not interested. His desire was for Eastern to be the largest air carrier in the free world. I think this yearning clouded his decisions. The debt created buying new equipment put the company in such an economic hole, it was doomed no matter what the unions did.

Borman issued a monthly letter to the pilots in which he suggested ways to improve operations. Without airline piloting experience, he made some mistakes, and his credibility began to dwindle. One recommendation he made, "When there are thunderstorms on control 1150 (a direct course between Palm Beach and Wilmington, NC, that has danger areas on both sides), it is better to fly through the storms than to penetrate the danger areas close by". This caused much apprehension among pilots. It was determined, there was no activity in these areas for weeks on end and they remained closed. I understand this problem is still with us today.

My committee made an exhaustive study of the proposed operation of the A-300 at DCA and found it just did not fit. The wet runway landing stop distance, derived from an actual test, exceeded FAR (Federal Aviation Regulations) requirements. The approach to Runway 18 could not be made without making a steep turn, and developing a high sink rate at a very low altitude. The takeoff performance to the north, with an engine failure, presented totally unacceptable performance and procedures. I told Borman, "If I made an approach like that in MIA, the FAA would lift my license for reckless operation." He snapped back, "That airplane is going into Washington no matter what you think." I had the distinct feeling he would liked to hit me.

When an aircraft loses power on takeoff, procedure requires a straight out climb, unless there is an published alternate procedure. The Washington National Airport has no alternate takeoff procedure for this runway. This was a time when reduced power takeoffs were introduced. Reduced power takeoffs lessen performance. Thus, decreasing clearance between you and obstructions. Previously, I had written a letter concerning DCA takeoff requirements. See letters below:

Mr. Langhorn Bond, December 1, 1978
Administrator National Headquarters
Federal Aviation Administration
800 Independence Avenue,
S. W. Washington, D. C. 20591

Dear Mr. Bond:

Five years ago a problem was brought before the FAA that has to date not been resolved. In the last two years I personally have tried in vain to have the FAA correct this area of potential disaster. I hope that an appeal to the Administrator will be the end of my quest to improve this area of airline safety.

Federal Air Regulations require that aircraft operated by air carriers meet take off performance criteria that is sufficient to clear all obstructions existing in the take-off area in the event an engine failure occurs during this critical period. This regulation is not being complied with!

When a pilot encounters an engine failure on take-off, he is required

(by Special Federal Aviation Regulation 422 B) to climb on the runway heading until clearing all obstructions in the take off area, or in the case of an alternate take off procedure is used, the pilot is limited to a 15 degree bank. This take off area being the horizontal area 300 feet either side of the extended runway centerline. On some runways, this area extends only 10,000 feet from the departure end of the runway. The obstructions outside this area are not plotted. Even the obstructions that are plotted within the take off area may not be plotted when considering the climb capabilities of fully loaded aircraft. Airline pilots as well as FAA Air Carrier Inspectors have been inadequately trained in this procedure.

While this problem is common to all aircraft and all airports, let us consider the take off of a DC-9 at Washington National Airport on runway 36 where no take off alternate exists. A pilot experiencing an engine failure at lift off here would probably attempt a climb out over the river as all departures are planned in this direction. A pilot who was properly trained would execute a straight out climb which, in all probability, would place him into an area of unknown obstructions.

The reason that he would be placed into this area being the minimum engine out climb gradient required of the DC-9 is 60:1 (6000 feet horizontal a climb of 100 feet is possible) while the obstructions below a 34:1 gradient are not plotted. With this in mind the properly trained pilot would find himself one mile from the departure end of the runway at an altitude of 100 feet surrounded by obstructions 175 feet high.

In the early days of jet operation, a system was devised and used, that plotted these obstructions and protected the public from this danger. This system was set aside several years ago in favor of the present system (34:1 plotting) with the public and most pilots unaware of the dangers involved.

It is my hope that you, as Administrator, are in a position to accomplish affirmative action in returning the air carriers and agency to a responsible and safe operation in this area. Sincerely,

Clyde Roach, Chairman OAT Committee

CR: vj V,

cc: Senator Howard Cannon Captain Lloyd Anderson OAT Committee

Mr. Edward Cook

Colonel Frank Borman

Clyde E. Roach

After the demonstration flights, the flight data recorder (FDR) was removed and read. Readings from one approach confirmed an unacceptable operation. When it was pointed out that the wet runway stop distance was equal to the length of the runway plus 500 feet, the gross weight manuals which contained the data, disappeared. The manuals reappeared two weeks later with revised numbers. All of a sudden, the airplane's capability to stop on a wet runway was enhanced. For certification purposes wet runway stop distance may be derived from either of two methods, an actual test, or by determining a braking coefficient to be used in a formula that generates stop distance. Of course, from a pilot's standpoint, the actual test is preferred. Politics is sometimes more significant than safety.

Borman hosted a meeting in Miami to persuade the 18-member MEC of the feasibility of the operation. In attendance; besides the MEC, were Borman, his staff, and representatives of the aircraft manufacturer and their test pilots. Their chief test pilot was later killed while flying an A-300. Evidently he was unable to disconnect auto pilot and throttles on a low flyby.

There were about 100 people in a large room at a Miami hotel. The main presentation, given by Walt Brady, centered on the comparison of the FDR readout of a DC-9 approach, and that of our A-300 approach projected on a giant screen in the form of charts. The implication was that if the DC-9 was safe, so must be the A-300. From the FDR you could get a picture of the approach path over the ground, with the airspeed, heading, altitude and sink rate. Comparisons of the two airplanes on the screen were quite compatible. Trouble is, the A-300 readout was not of the flight I witnessed. I told the company, "We are studying the performance of the A-300. At a later date, if you like, we can examine the DC-9 performance."

At DCA I was in the cockpit as Captain Preissner made the first approach, a VOR (Visual Omni Range) approach. He crossed the final approach fix 400 feet below the minimum crossing altitude.

Immediately after landing, I advised Bill that the approach was illegal and dangerous, and the approach would have to be repeated.

The next approach, accomplished according to proper procedures, produced a steep turn and high sink rate at a very low altitude. This approach was never mentioned in the presentation. In a deliberate attempt to deceive the pilots, the company was using data from the first approach. They had data from other approaches but did not let the pilots observe. During the meeting, I called attention to this glaring misrepresentation The company continued the show as if I had said nothing. Later I went to the front, and with a long stick pointed to the chart and said to the MEC, "Maybe you guys didn't understand what I said before. This is not the chart for the illegal approach, which I have already told you about." I think this wrecked the company presentation.

I asked the chief pilot to explain the test that produced wet runway stop distance. His explanation; the airplane was maneuvered to the threshold at Vref.. Maximum braking was applied before touchdown. I then asked, what was the sink rate at the threshold? His answer, "1000' per minute". Any pilot knows, this is as close to an accident as you can get. A sink rate of 1000 feet a minute at the threshold is such a violation of common sense, it is enough to ground any pilot. My next question, "Was the airplane flyable after that?" There was some laughter.

The FAA waived some safety regulations pertaining to the operation, but the pilots saw through the sham, and refused to fly the A-300 into DCA. If the pilots didn't approve, the application was doomed. I wanted to approve the operation. The company could have made lots of money. But, it just didn't fit my idea of safety. There is no such thing as complete safety. You are not completely safe in bed at home. It's a matter of how much risk are you willing to take.

One good thing did come of this. On the departure end of the north runway, part of the bay was filled in, lengthening the overrun area. Subsequently, one of our B-727s aborted a takeoff and stopped on the newly created overrun. Under previous conditions, he would have been in the bay.

Shortly after my retirement, EAL pilots voted to approve the operation, but it was too late. After a personal observation of the approach, the Director of the FAA banned the operation. The FAA received a copy of my report, as did the Senate Aviation Subcommittee. The A-300 was not, and is still not, approved for operation into DCA. For my work on this project, I am very proud.

A DC-9 simulator, programmed at max gross weight for a takeoff on this runway, with an engine failure at critical speed, made the normal left turn departure up the river. The simulation resulted in a crash into the bridge. No records were kept, nor was the information passed on. A straight out departure, which he should have made, might have destroyed the Washington Monument. More information not passed on.

Subsequent to the simulation, in 1982 an Air Florida B-737, taking off on the same runway, experienced a power loss. The aircraft hit the bridge, and crashed with multiple fatalities. Cause of the accident; failure of the crew to turn on the engine anti-ice system produced an erroneous, abnormally high indication of power output. The power was available, but the crew failed to push the throttles forward enough.

All simulators I have been exposed to had a switch to simulate engine ice. Students were taught how to recognize and handle the occurrence. I have often wondered if this crew had the benefit of this training.

I thought this accident would produce some action on the issue of takeoff performance. Thinking back, I should not have expected any action. The deficiency had been recognized since 1973, and nothing had been done. As recently as 1996 I questioned two Delta captains about their DCA takeoff procedures. They confirmed that the same conditions still exist. In 1980 I questioned 45 captains, check captains and FAA inspectors as to the proper procedure when taking off to the north with an engine failure. All except five gave the wrong answer. Certainly, I don't expect any changes at this late date. So next time you takeoff on Runway 36 at DCA, Good Luck! With the arrival of more powerful jet engines, takeoff performance has been enhanced. Maybe, this is one reason for lack of interest in the subject. But, the DC-9 still operates at DCA.

We maintained B-727 service to Martinique in the Carribean, day and night. With an engine failure on takeoff, a straight out climb would not clear the mountains. The alternate takeoff procedure (limited to a 15 degree bank) also would not clear the mountains. This was determined by an actual flight. For night operation, light beacons on the ground were supposed to pinpoint the course required to miss the mountains. The lights were not maintained and were seldom visible. Confirmed by tower controllers. Performance engineers still maintained performance was adequate. Slipstick results don't necessarily insure safety. I continue to read about aircraft, in less developed countries, flying into mountains. But, it can happen anyplace.

Eastern Airlines operated, probably, the largest airline training facility in the world, and I think the best. We trained, not only our pilots, but pilots of other airlines in the USA, and from around the world. In addition, we trained people of various other occupations. At one time, over 100 instructors, flight and ground, were assigned. Our takeoff and landings totaled as much as 350 per day. One year, the training department turned a profit greater than the airline.

The building, latest state of the art, would seat 1000 students. The rooms were small and well equipped. Each student had an electronic means of answering questions and a view of a large projection screen. The underlying theme seemed to be, "No one leaves the room without all the correct information." When a test was given, and the student gave the wrong answer, the process was stopped until the student exhibited correct knowledge of the subject. No one left the room without all the information. I don't know why this technique was never adopted by the public school system.

CHAPTER TEN
WEATHER

As OAT (Operations and Training) committee chairman, I attended a presentation put on by three NASA physicists for the purpose of disseminating information gained from a study of thunderstorms in Florida. Florida was chosen for the study because more tornados occur here than in any other State. Having the most thunderstorms means the most tornados. Our tornadoes are generally not as severe as those of the Midwest.

Expenses for the entire show were paid by the ALPA. The study conducted in central Florida, revealed valuable new information on wind shear and micro burst. Wind shear is the sudden change of velocity, and or, direction of wind currents. A micro burst is a high speed descending column of air coming from the bottom of a thunderstorm. The column of air, on contact with the ground, is dispersed in horizontal directions at high velocity, and is often mistaken for a tornado. The column of descending air may come straight down, or on a slant.

Early in the presentation, the speaker said, "Everything we tell you can be proven." Then came the statement, "No commercial jet in landing configuration can penetrate a micro burst without crashing, and furthermore, any afternoon thunderstorm is capable of producing a micro burst." One photograph taken from directly overhead a sugarcane field was quite impressing. The picture exhibiting the aftermath of a micro burst, taken from directly over a sugarcane field. The area was flattened in a perfect circle. The stalks were completely flattened, like a heavy weight had been dropped on each. All lay on the ground pointing away from the center of the circle.

Sitting next to me was Tom Button, Vice President of flight operations. I gave him an elbow punch in the ribs, and said, "Tom, that's what I want to talk to you about when this is over."

Another statement was forthcoming. "Many tornadoes reported in the press are not tornadoes. They are micro burst." Front page pictures in an Orlando newspaper were exhibited, showing damage from 'last night's tornado'. NASA technology, painting the area at the time, proved the damage resulted from a micro burst. The tornado funnel cloud always forms in the non-rain area under the thunderstorm. I guess, in the absence of an eye witness, or if the damage occurs during rain, it was a micro burst and not a tornado.

The charts did prove that any jet penetrating a micro burst at a normal approach speed might crash. During the question and answer session I asked, "What would be the effect of 20 or 30 knots extra airspeed at the time of penetration." The speaker answered, "This might prevent an accident."

In a subsequent meeting with Tom and his staff, I suggested that the information learned from NASA be passed on to the pilots. Also, that a blurb be added to the operations manual relieving the captain of any responsibility of conforming to any profile or airspeed when wind shear is suspected. I was told, "The pilots would shut down half the airline every summer. They wouldn't go near a thunderstorm." So, the pilots were kept in the dark again.

Delta didn't advise their pilots of the new data and subsequently lost an L-1011 making an approach to Dallas in close proximity to a thunderstorm. Flight data recordings proved the flight encountered a micro burst or wind shear at normal approach speed. I don't believe the pilots would have made that approach had they been apprized of the NASA findings. Or, at least, they would have carried some extra speed.

Some things I have learned that may be worthy of remembering. You can't have a thunderstorm without lightening. You can have lightening without a thunderstorm. You can't have a severe tornado without a thunderstorm. Although, I have witnessed waterspouts under small cumulus clouds, so small no rain was present. On the prairies they have dust devils with no cloud formation. There are no thunderstorms in the eye wall of a hurricane. Any afternoon thunderstorm is capable of generating a micro burst.

Having lived my long life in Miami, hurricanes were familiar. To fly the Caribbean in the summertime was even more enlightening. A captain flying a Miami-San Juan turnaround, two days in a row penetrated the eye of a hurricane. He made announcements to the passengers revealing his intentions. He was called on the carpet in the chief pilot's office for scaring hell out of passengers.

Hurricanes do not produce turbulence (in the tight circulation) as extreme as that produced by thunderstorms, mainly because winds in a hurricane are horizontal, in a thunderstorm both vertical and horizontal. Before our airplanes were equipped with radar, we flew through thunderstorms, hurricanes or whatever else happened to be on course. Eastern once received a complaint from the US Weather Service in the Washington, DC area. All altitudes were occupied By Eastern airplanes. Hurricane hunters couldn't get a clearance.

Once, flying a Connie, I was listening to a commercial broadcast of hurricane information. They had the hurricane centered over Cedar Key, Florida. At 21,000 feet we broke out in the eye, with smooth air, bright sunlight, and Cedar Key straight down. The eye wall produced heavy, but not severe turbulence. On another flight at 6,000 feet near New Orleans, with winds of 120 knots, it was so smooth that seat belts were not needed.

The most severe turbulence associated with hurricanes is in bands of thunderstorms on the outer edge. Tornadoes are produced only by thunderstorms and there are no thunderstorms in the eye-wall of a hurricane. Some people think I am wrong in this belief. But my experience tells me otherwise. In discussions with meteorologist, I like to ask, "Have you ever heard thunder in the tight circulation of a hurricane?" No one had. Downed power lines and shorted transformers produce the flashes of light and sound that are misidentified as lightning. One encyclopedia defines the eye wall of a hurricane as a tightly packed circle of thunderstorms. If this were true, you would be able to read a newspaper at midnight by the light of continuous lightening. Imagine circular winds of a tornado inside the tight circulation of a hurricane. On one side of the tornado, wind would be in the opposite direction of that of the hurricane. It does not happen. Try drawing isobaric lines of a tornado inside a hurricane. I have observed the eye of hurricanes from the ground at least four times. Hurricane hunters have rarely observed lightning when penetrating the eye.

Even the most trusted sources of information, are sometimes in error. The World Book Encyclopedia defines CAT as, clear air turbulence. CAT is associated with small temperature changes. If we could detect changes far ahead of the airplane, it would be of great help. The article explains a successful attempt to predict CAT ahead of an airplane in flight. Eastern Airlines provided the airplane for the test. Air Force provided the meteorologist. The experiment was a total failure. I flew the Constellation on the test flight that was supposed to prove success. Don't let authorized sources convince you of an untruth.

Airplanes are struck by lightning and discharge the bolt frequently, without any ill affects. Our fleet of DC-3's, which didn't have static arresters, displayed the evidence (small holes in the fabric-covered elevators or discolorations on aluminum surfaces). That was during a time when we penetrated thunderstorms on a daily basis. In flight, when you hear the thunder simultaneously with the lighting flash, your airplane has probably been struck. I happened to be looking out the window when a lightning bolt discharged from the #4 prop on a DC-7. A muffled explosion was heard as it burned off four inches on one prop blade. A strange odor permeated the cockpit for a few seconds. When you see a lightening bolt, it is impossible to tell where it originated (cloud to ground or ground to cloud). But it always travels from + to a

- charge. This gives concern to the new aircraft made with composites. How well will they handle natural electrical happenings?

I've been in thunderstorms which produced turbulence that made it impossible to control the aircraft. Altitude variations were as much as 10,000 feet. Before the use of radar, more aircraft were lost due to thunderstorms than any other cause. Airspeed is the most important factor in turbulence. All airplanes have a turbulent penetrating speed. It is usually the speed at which maximum deflection of any control surface will not over stress the airplane (maneuvering speed–VA). But, you gotta remember, gust loads are increased by the <u>square</u> of the increase in airspeed. Let your airspeed increase and gust loads jump like crazy.

Before I learned any of this stuff, while still in service flying C-47 -- from my autobiography -- On the way back to Natal, taking off from Boriquin field in Port Rico, a huge thunderstorm engulfed the island. Climbing out after takeoff, cockpit conservation was about these storms. Neither of us had ever been in one. In Cadet training, I don't remember anyone mentioning thunderstorms. We decided to explore.

From clear smooth air outside the storm, I turned and entered at about six thousand feet. Immediately we encountered moderate turbulence and heavy rain. It was difficult to maintain a wings level attitude, and we were climbing awfully fast. Then it really got rough. Lightning was so close, you could hear the thunder. With saint elmos fire dancing across the windshield, the airplane was uncontrollable. I don't know how high we went because I couldn't read the altimeter. We probably were not in the storm more than a couple of minutes but it seemed an eternity. We were tossed out the side at about 15,000 feet, like a child throwing a toy airplane. That airplane will not climb much higher. From that time on, I had great respect for thunderstorms.

A hurricane was approaching Miami. Some of the squall lines had already passed. The airport was experiencing heavy rain, high winds, and was already closed. All airplanes that could not be protected in hangars had been flown out of Miami, except one B-720. Someone had miscalculated required hangar floor space. his one had to be flown out late.

The company called me with the urgent message, "Please come fly it out as soon as possible."

"Have the airplane fueled and pre-flighted." I replied, "I'll be there in 20 minutes." I left my family in our secured house and made the quick trip to the airport. The streets were deserted and most traffic signal lights didn't work. Some trees and power lines were down.

The other two crew members, whom I Didn't recognize, were walking in the gate as I arrived. Without delay we taxied to Runway 9L. On the way out, my neighbor, the only controller on duty, advised, "Wind 020 at 50 gusting to 70."

"We need a clearance to Jacksonville." My copilot replied. I could see he was a little nervous. From the controller, "You got it. Ain't no one else flying today. Runway heading go when you want." In those days the controllers were professional servants and they did an admirable job. Airports were not closed by ground personnel.

The takeoff was bumpy, but we were in smooth air shortly. We spent a few hours in Jacksonville until the brunt of the storm turned to miss Miami, then returned home.

There is currently an intense scientific debate on hurricanes. Some scientists hypothesize Global Warming is making tropical storms more common and intense. Fact is, hurricanes are not more common or more severe. Hurricanes are identified and category rated by only one yardstick, sustained wind. Some metrologists consider lowest barometric pressure. The method of measuring sustained wind was changed about 50 years ago. When comparing recent hurricanes with those of the past, meteorologist, and others arguing the case, are not aware and do not take into consideration the change. This has been confirmed by NOAA.

Up until the 1950s, the method for deriving wind speed was to observe an anemometer for three minutes. Sustained wind was recorded as the lowest reading over the time period. Gusts were recorded as the highest reading on the scale during the same period. Today a more sophisticated method is used. In the United States, we measure the wind every five seconds, and then average 24 measurements (2 minutes) together to get the sustained wind speed. Wind gusts are reported as the highest 5 second average. This formula is used regardless of the method of observation, anemometer, Doppler radar, aircraft, ect.. Doppler radar can only measure wind in rain areas, and then not too accurately.

Assume you are measuring wind in a hurricane with an anemometer. Steady wind is 100MPH. For 5 seconds, wind increases to 150MPH. Another short gust registers 130. Under the old method, recorded wind would be 100 with gust to 150. This a category 1 hurricane. With the new method, recorded sustained wind would be considerably higher, and would be called a category 2, or maybe a 3. You can readily see, the newer method inflates sustained wind by using gusts. The new method automatically ups the category of all storms. Anyone who has experienced a hurricane on the ground is aware of the extreme difference in sustained wind and gusts.

If you haven't seen a UFO, keep flying and you probably will. Most of the old timers I know have seen something that could not be explained.

Over the Atlantic in clear air, at 33,000 feet in a DC-8, I was recovering a dropped pencil on the glare shield. To recover, movement required me to lean far forward. With my head near the windshield, looking straight up, I saw something really strange. A colorful egg shaped pattern the width of the cockpit was stationary. The colors, light green, pink, and blue, were separated by distinct vertical lines. I exclaimed to the copilot, "Look at this!" At first he couldn't see anything. But, when he put his head up close to the windshield, looking up, he too saw it.

When I withdrew my head to a normal position, whatever it was, was gone. I don't know what prompted me to do what I did next. With my head in the same position where it was when the object was seen, I switched off the autopilot hold switch. Then, gently varied altitude up and down about 50 feet off the original altitude. The image reappeared. That's when I realized we were flying in a very thin layer of ice crystals. Generally, when flying in ice crystals, the little specks flash by millions per second. These crystals were so sparse only two or three per second were seen. Unless you were looking straight up, they were invisible.

Fully intending to report the incident. I drew sketches and made notes. I don't remember why I never made the report.

My friend, Shipe Childs, reported a UFO sighting similar to the one described above. He told me if he had it to do over again, he would not report it. Shipes' sighting is one of the few still listed as unexplained in many publications.

I think one possible explanation for some UFO sightings is sunlight refracted through ice crystals, like sunlight refracted to cause a rainbow. This is the process that causes a halo around the sun. Occasionally, the halo appears around the moon. Rapid movement and contour of UFOs might be explained by secondary reflection, and or, by rapid break up and reformation of ice crystals. Maybe looking through the windshield at such an obtuse angle had something to do with my sighting. In any case, we should not jump to conclusions.

There was the night over Norfolk Va., people on the ground, and pilots, reported strange lights flashing all over. On a trip from San Juan to Miami, up high up ahead, what appeared to be a vertical stationary searchlight beam, never moved. We flew very close to the shaft of light. Looking down, it appeared to originate about 10,000 feet below and fade away 10,000 feet above. I have seen lots of searchlight during the war. This was not real.

On a night training flight out of Miami, I was at 35,000 feet about half way between Key Biscayne and Andros island. We were on a northerly heading when the copilot said, "What's that?" A bright light was coming right at us at the same altitude. On training flights, it was common to receive a block instrument clearance. My clearance was from 15,000' to 35,000' between Key Biscayne VOR radials of 090 and 180, for 100 miles. I called the center and ask if we had traffic. It was a missile just fired from Cape Carnival.

CHAPTER ELEVEN
MOTHER'S DAY 1966

There were a large number of pilots to be trained. When the air traffic around Miami International Airport became too heavy, the company moved the 727 flight training to Ft. Worth, Texas. Talk about the crowded sky. At this time the new Tamiami airport had more takeoffs and landings than in all of Europe. American Airlines did our maintenance at Love Field in Dallas, and we flew out of the old Greater Southwest Airport, just a few miles away. Pilots stayed at the Great Western Motel nearby.

I had been at Ft. Worth for a month or two as instructor and check captain. On Mothers Day 1966, Captain Bud Fisher was to get his rating ride. At the motel before daylight, I met Bud, John Stone, (flight engineer instructor), and Mr. Gene Breece, the FAA inspector. We had breakfast at a nearby restaurant and took the limo to Love Field to pick up the airplane.

The airplane was number 102. American had been working on the landing gear all night. The night before, walking through the maintenance area, I witnessed a mechanic pounding the main landing gear with a heavy hammer, and made some snide remark like, "They are trying to destroy our airplane."

On a rating ride the FAA inspector is the judge of acceptable performance. The check captai in the right seat, is the safety pilot, and responsible for the flight. I gave Mr. Breece my standard briefing, the same to all inspectors, "Don't pull any circuit breakers without first checking with me and don't talk to the pilot while he is flying." Then Mr. Breece gave Bud a briefing as what to expect. No one briefed me on what was going to happen. If they had, I wouldn't have gone.

It was still dark as we made our first takeoff. The first landing was to be at Greater Southwest Airport. On final approach, Bud called, "Gear down and final checklist." I put the gear handle down, and observed green lights on the mains, but the nose gear indicating system was all screwed up. I knew the nose wheel did not go down, because there was no sound of the doors opening. I told Bud, "Make a missed approach." At a safe altitude, I recycled the gear twice with the same results. Then I told John, "Take a look at it," A viewing port in the floor allows a visual check. He reported, "It's up tight as a drum."

Flying from the right seat, I made a steep turn to increase the G-load, and rapidly moved the gear handle from up to down without pausing at the off position. I found out later; this produces a hammering effect, rather than a push. The landing gear went down, all of them, with a loud explosive-type sound and a moderate thump to the airframe. Red lights appeared on the left main gear-indicating system. The nose wheel indication was still screwed up and one hydraulic system had failed. I asked Breece to go back and take a look. From the cabin windows some of the gear is visible. While he was gone Bud and I changed seats, so there would be no question as to who was in command.

Breece appeared frightened, and reported a large hole in the top of the left wing. I advised him that he was now part of the crew, and that I wanted any suggestions or comments he might have, and no hindsight. Then John had a look. His comments were to the effect, "It don't look good."

Using the remaining hydraulic system, I raised the landing gear. The nose and right main retracted normally. Then I went back to have a look myself. The hole in the top of the wing was about the size of a jeep, with jagged pieces of skin sticking up. The gear actuating cylinder, about the size of a small telephone pole eight feet long, had failed at the outboard attach point, and was askew. The landing gear was down, but the side brace was broken and the wheels were not in line with the airframe. Worst of all, a steady stream of hydraulic fluid was trailing back off the wing. I immediately yelled up to John, "Cut off the other pump." It was too late. The reservoir was empty. Now we were in manual reversion on the ailerons, which means restricted roll control. In such a situation the elevators are not affected, but the rudders are inoperative, and there is no way to get them back. One rudder has a backup system, but requires fluid from one of the main systems. I knew if I used it, any remaining fluid would be pumped overboard.

The next three hours were spent trying to get help from any source. Miami tech-service, contacted by radio, suggested I G-load the airplane, and try to force the gear down. I replied, "You must not have been listening. I tried that. That's when the SOB tore up."

Another training flight, flown by J.B. Marsh, pulled up alongside to view the damage. He reported only what we already knew. I asked him to look at the whole airplane for other damage. None was found.

I had plenty of fuel, since we always started with almost full tanks. The company wanted the airplane in Miami for maintenance reasons. When I asked for a fuel burn-off to Miami, with the left gear down and a big hole in the wing, they said, "Forget it."

Tulsa, Oklahoma was suggested for a landing because of American's large maintenance base there. I had been circling Carswell Air Force Base, A SAC (Strategic Air Command) base, in case an immediate landing became necessary. Now, to please the company, I was on the way to Tulsa. The company didn't want the airplane on a SAC base because if an airplane blocks the active runway, a cable is attached to the airplane, and if the runway is needed, it would be dragged or bulldozed off the runway.

About half way to Tulsa the airport manager sent me a message, "We don't have enough foam for both the runway and the airplane." He suggested use of a short crosswind runway so I wouldn't close his airport. That sealed my decision to land at Carswell. I reversed course and told Bud to advise the company. Airport managers are not necessarily versed in safety.

I switched my radio to Carswell tower and asked to speak with the officer of the day. My first question, "What's this about bulldozing my airplane off the runway?"

"Oh, we won't do that unless we have a red alert." When asked to define a red alert, he answered, "An actual war."

I told the crew, "If we have a war, I don't care what they do with this airplane." This was during the Cold War with Russia. When asked what length of the runway should be foamed, I replied, "All you can spare. If I have to land with no flaps, minimum speed is 180 knots. She will slide forever."

I learned later that Captain "Robby" Robins was asked by the crash crew what length of the runway should be foamed. He told me he had absolutely no idea how much would be needed. When pressed for an answer, off the top of his head he answered, "3500 feet." That proved to be exactly right. After it was over, a crash crew member said, "That Captain Robins sure knows his foam."

One Eastern B-727 had landed with the landing gear up at Miami on a foamed runway. Using full reverse power, he still slid about 4500 feet. But it didn't appear that we could make the slow approach that he made.

In preparing for the landing, I told John to dump fuel until it stopped draining and mark the time. This way we would know exactly how much fuel remained. Using the fuel flow gages (fuel flow gages are touted to be the most accurate gages in the cockpit), I planned to land with as little fuel as possible. Also, I needed a landing card for no flaps and full flaps.

The next order of business was to try and get some wing flaps. Using the electrical system, I called for two degrees. Two flight spoilers on the left wing were floating and five leading edge devices did not deploy. With manual ailerons, the roll to the left was uncontrollable, even with asymmetrically power. I yelled "Take em up!" That's when I began to wish we had parachutes.

In my briefing to the crew, I had already explained what could happen on landing. Essentially, with a touchdown on the broken left main gear, when and if the tires blew, the strut would dig in and we would cartwheel to the left. More probably, when I ran out of aileron, the right wing would dig in and we would cartwheel to the right. I told John and Mr. Breece, only Bud and I would be in the cockpit, adding, "Sit anywhere you like. If we catch fire, it won't amount to much, as we are just about out of everything that will burn."

Even though the last hydraulic reservoir showed empty, and I knew when the pump was powered any fluid left would start squirting again, I had to try. The DC-8 hydraulic gage, when showing empty, has plenty left, but not this one. I notified the tower we were on a long final, and just about out of fuel. The crash crew cleared the runway, even though they were not quite finished with the foaming. With no rudder, ailerons were a prime concern. I told Bud to power the ailerons. They worked fine, so there had to be some hydraulic fluid left. Next I called for wing flaps two degrees, then five degrees, and then full flaps. We were about 500 feet now, and I never even thought of looking at the hydraulic quantity gauge. All leading edge devices extended properly. The hydraulic system was working fine. The roll control problem, now caused by floating spoilers, was manageable. Although, almost full ailerons were required to maintain wings level. Had there not been enough fluid for those last two minutes, the ailerons would have reverted to manual, and we would have rolled over and bought the farm.

As I closed the throttles to decelerate, the landing gear warning horn sounded. With all the time and planing put into this, we had forgotten to deactivate the warning system. John came running up from the rear with a smile on his face, and pulled the circuit breaker. I wondered what else I had forgotten. There was no check lists to cover this.

We must have been a site for the soldiers watching an airliner on final approach with only one twisted landing gear down, and sheets of metal sticking up on top of one wing.

Clyde E. Roach

Now my concern was, did I wait too long to start the approach? Was there enough fuel to reach the runway? The swath of foam, visible down the center of the runway was only 60 feet wide. It looked more like a painted center line. I wasn't even sure of putting the airplane in the foam, much less keeping it there. It goes without saying – this was, by far, the most horrendous sweat job of my life. At about 100 feet I yanked the gear handle up. If that broken gear retracted, I felt we could make it. Over the threshold, with the throttles closed, our airspeed less than 100 knots. Bud pulled all the engine fire shutoff switches. Now we were committed to momentum. That hunk of iron was going where it was aimed. There was not much I could do to control destiny.

Touchdown in the first 50 feet of foam on the broken left main landing gear was smooth. About 1500 feet down the runway, in spite of full ailerons, the right wing tip was about to touch the ground. I heard and felt a muffled bang (both tires on the broken gear had blown, even in the slippery foam. What we had been hoping for happened. The gear folded and we settled on the belly. Sliding straight down the center of runway, we stopped with 100 feet of foam still ahead.

Too much can't be said for the efficiency of the SAC crash crew. Within seconds after we came to a stop, the cockpit was covered with foam squirted from a truck that had been waiting at the end of the foam. I opened the side window and signaled them to hold off. If we didn't have a fire now, we would not have one.

The whole episode lasted four hours, and one TV station filmed the landing for the national news that night. The chairman of the NTSB accident investigation team was sitting in his car off the end of the runway, watching the show. He had heard the news of my predicament on the radio while driving to work. He was the first person I met after jumping from the front door. Stairs were not needed, since the plane was resting on its belly. We shook hands and he congratulated me for a job well done. Then advised me that he would be in charge of the investigation.

While sitting in a staff car near the runway with some Air Force officers, reporters surrounded the car, trying to get an interview. Someone asked if I would like to make a phone call. "Yes, I said, I'd like to call Rick Rivenbark (vice president of flight operations), but on Mothers Day, it may be hard to get through." The SAC's communication system is as good as the crash crew. Within seconds I was talking to Rick. I wanted to report the outcome and ask how to handle the media.

He said, "I can't tell you what to say, but you have to talk to them."

During this fiasco Thad Royal, in charge of B-727 training in Miami, called my wife, Roxie, while we were still in the air, to let her know what was going on. I thought this was an astute thing to do. That afternoon Thad and Roxie, with some mechanics arrived in Dallas. My crew, minus Mr. Breece, met with the NTSB, and gave a preliminary statement. I told Bud and John, "With the FAA looking over our shoulder, no use trying to cover up anything. Just tell it like it happened."

That night, after watching myself on national news, Roxie and I went to a nearby steak house for dinner. There were a lot of pilots there. As we walked in, they gave us an ovation. I Didn't feel like a hero. I was just thankful to be alive--again.

ALPA policy is never to testify before the NTSB without legal representation. I asked various people for advice on the subject. Rick said, "You are management, and if you are in trouble, so are we." Thad said, "Don't worry, if they ground you, we will pay your salary and you can sit at home." I thought the only thing that might have been done wrong was dumping fuel at a low altitude (1500 feet). Later I learned there is no minimum altitude for dumping fuel.

The flight data recorder revealed my airspeed to be much higher than it should have been when I was G-loading the airplane trying to extend the nose gear, but no one seemed to care. Maybe I should have been wearing my half-eye glasses. I started wearing glasses for near vision when flying the Constellation. On night flights I couldn't read the radio frequency on the dial located on the overhead panel. Before the first takeoff I would set the frequency, and thereafter count the clicks to change frequency. This worked fine until the copilot selected a new frequency. Then I was lost. I had to wear the half-eye glasses upside down in order to see above.

Within two days I received an official notice of the NTSB hearing to be held at Carswell Air Force Base. I was allowed to bring only one person with me. I asked Thad to go.

At the hearing, in a large impressive room, seated around a long polished mahogany table, were about 15 people. The only one I knew was the chairman, seated at the head of the table. Thad and I took the chairs waiting for us.

The meeting opened with the FAA representative passing out copies of the electrical schematic of the nose landing gear warning system. His implication was, since I had not made a fly by of the tower to confirm the position of the nose-gear, there was no way I could have known if it was up or down. So, I caused my own problem. I could see right away that they were out to get me. I began to regret not having a lawyer.

While the airplane was still on the runway, after being jacked up in preparation for moving, someone pried open the nose gear doors. This precluded any possibility of determining why they didn't open in flight. At this point in time, we had not much experience with this problem. Years later, I learned there had been over 100 industry-wide incidents of nose-gear malfunction. Nose-gear door rigging was the culprit. Nose gear door up latches must be open to allow landing gear up latches to unlock.

I wrote a procedure to help pilots handle this type emergency, and asked the company to insert it in the operations manual. There is a way to land the B-727 with the nose-gear up and hold the nose off until the airplane almost comes to a stop. It encompasses the use of outboard spoilers only. I have demonstrated the action many times.

Turn off the inboard spoilers. Now when you use the speed brake, only outboard spoilers will be deflected. Since the outboard spoilers are aft of the airplane pivot point, they work just like an elevator. Use of outboard spoilers are required when making a jammed stabilizer landing. Elevator control may not be sufficient, depending where the stabilizer jammed.

Not being an electrical engineer, I refused comment on the schematic. However, I did explain how, from the sound, extension of the nose-gear is positive. Never having heard of this, the Board wanted a demonstration. In training, students are required to manually crank down the landing gear, one at a time. I had observed and listened to the procedure a few dozen times.

The next day an FAA representative accompanied me on a flight for proof. The flight engineer cranked down the nose gear first. The sound of the doors opening into the air stream was quite loud. Then you could hear the gear coming out and a thump when it locked. Next, a main gear was cranked down. Since it was so far aft, you had to listen intently to hear anything at all. The FAA said, "I'm convinced, let's go home."

B-727's are still being flown, and I wonder if the pilots are alerted to listen. I know the simulators are not programmed for the correct sound.

The accident was caused by the failure of American Airline mechanics to install a bearing in the outboard attach point of the left main landing gear actuator. The bearing softens energy exerted on structure. The part was found on the ground where they had been working the night before. American Airlines paid a fine, and two mechanics were disciplined. A Boeing representative told of the same type failure occurring on an airplane on jacks in the hangar, because of the same part had been left out. The same type damage occurred. When the actuating cylinder broke and flipped upward, it missed the aileron cable by only an inch. Had the cylinder contacted the aileron cable, the airplane would have rolled over and crashed. Sometimes a force beyond our perception takes over.

Damage to the aircraft caused by the landing was minimal. The mechanics told me if it wasn't for the damage that occurred in flight, with installation of new wing flaps, the airplane could have been flown out that day. This airplane makes a beautiful wheels-up landing. But I wonder about the new wide body airplanes with wing-mounted engines that extend below the fuselage. Sooner or later, a wide body will have to land with the gear up. It will not be a belly landing. It will be an engine landing.

Eastern mechanics cut a section of the wing flaps that had been ground down as we slid along the runway, and presented it to me as a memento. The TV station sent me a 16-mm copy of the landing and interview. I had an 8-mm copy made for home use, and gave the original to the company for use in training.

Years later, my son Steve, an FAA air traffic controller, had the FAA records in Oklahoma City searched for a copy of the accident report. Would you believe it? There is no record of this accident. Things are still as messed up as ever. I finally found a short record on the internet. It blamed me, the pilot.

Colonel Borman (the astronaut, now the CEO at Eastern) wrote me a letter of commendation which provoked a laugh. It was worded in a way that provided the company the right to discipline me if further investigation warranted.

CHAPTER TWELVE
D-DAY PLUS ONE

NORMANDY

A World War Two story you might find interesting —from my autobiography.

The midnight briefing disclosed a six-ship formation of C-47s carrying ammunition and medical supplies to a drop zone just a few miles north of the one we used the night before D-Day. Our entry point on the Cherbourg peninsular would be over Utah Beach.

Some paratroopers were cut off and needed ammunition and medical supplies. I would fly the number two spot (right wing of the lead airplane). Chain of command of a formation always transfers, if necessary, from the lead ship to the number two position.

My copilot on this mission, Lt. Scott, had previously flown fighters during the Battle of Britain before being transferred to bombers in the Eighth Air Force. Some bomber groups looked upon transfer to Troop Carrier as punishment. It might have been. He always seemed a bit weird to me, but our relationship was genial.

After the briefing, in the mess hall, the proverbial last meal was served. We always hoped for fresh eggs, but only once during my tour overseas were they served. This morning the fare was SOS (some unchaste pilots called it s---on a shingle), creamed corn beef on toast, which was one of my favorites.

My ship was loaded and waiting on the flight line. The load consisted of four para-racks hung under the belly that could be salvoed electrically from the cockpit. Each rack carried a bundle of supplies (weighing as much as 600 pounds each) with a parachute . In the cabin were six or eight para-bundles that would be shoved out the cargo door by my crew chief and radio operator. But the bundles were too heavy and bulky for two men to handle. The airplane was overloaded by any measure.

An intelligence officer arrived in a jeep with a private dressed in normal khaki and announced, "This guy is going with you. You will need help getting the bundles out". Our dress for combat missions was always the same, a flight suit with no visible rank or national identification. Each of us carried an escape kit with a fake passport and lots of counterfeit money, but no identification except dog tags. All of us carried a .45 caliber pistol, usually in a shoulder holster, and in the cabin were two "Tommy" guns. In briefing the private I learned he was from the quartermaster corps, had no weapons, and had never been up in an airplane before, much less been in combat. I didn't get his name. He was scarred to the point of terror. But, who wasn't?

The weather was lousy. Visibility, restricted by fog that choked your lungs, was practically nil. We were guided to the runway by jeeps. While waiting in takeoff position, a jeep rolled up alongside my cockpit. I opened my side window as the intelligence officer stood on the hood of the jeep and yelled, "For Gods sakes don't go the way you were briefed. They have moved a whole F------ German army into that area!" I wondered what I was supposed to do about that. There was only one way to get to the drop zone, straight in over Utah Beach. And besides, I was just going to follow my lead ship. I presume he warned the others.

With visibility less than 100 meters, it was an instrument takeoff for the lead ship, a formation takeoff for the rest of us. To maintain sight of the formation lights, the rest of us would have to keep it in extremely close. We made a true formation takeoff of two three-ship elements on a narrow runway under the most adverse conditions.

Roaring down the runway, the moisture laden air was ominous. As I called, "Landing gear up." Scott came back with, "Bank to the right.

Airspeed 90." My cockpit was no more than 20 feet from the wing tip of the lead airplane. "Bank increasing. Airspeed 80." The formation was supposed to climb straight out, but there was nothing I could do except try and hold my position. Our method of flying instrument formation was as follows: The pilot not flying kept up a running chat as to airspeed banking left or right, and descending or climbing. This, to some degree, helped in preventing vertigo.

As the bank became steeper and the airspeed lower, Scott's voice got louder and more distressed. The airplane began to shake. My leader was putting me, on the inside of a turn, into a stall. With full power I veered away from the leader. Flying on instruments, with the yoke in my lap, the airplane still shaking, the tail struck something on the ground accompanied by a terrific jolt. I never knew the damage because we didn't bring this one back. From now on, we were living on borrowed time. The stall recovery was slow due to weight and the para-racks attached to the belly. I doubt that anyone had ever stalled a C-47 with para-racks attached, or at this weight. We were alone now, and no way to find the other guys in this soup.

Climbing to 5000 feet, I called "Darkie" (code name for emergency assistance) on a common frequency, and was given a heading and distance to Utah Beach. Flying instruments in the dark with no outside lights, and only red lights in the cockpit, I wondered how many other airplanes were up here and about the chances of a midair collision. We encountered a severe bump in the smooth air. I knew we came dreadfully close to another airplane. The brilliance of a searchlight destroyed our night vision accommodation. Even lighting a cigarette had the same effect. Before the mission, we had worn red goggles for four hours. This was supposed to enhance night vision.

The weather began to break up as the sun began to brightened the partly cloudy sky. Over the English Channel two P-51 fighters appeared from nowhere and settled, one on each wing. Scott grinned, "Hey look. We got escorts." It was a good feeling to have company.

It was broad daylight when Utah Beach loomed dead ahead. I pushed the nose over, and with the throttles full forward, reduced full RPM slightly. I was going to cross that beach as fast as this unarmed airplane would go and as low as possible. Scott lit up a cigarette and offered me one. We smoked like fiends. "No. Not now." I responded.

"You better have one. It may be your last." To tell the truth, the thought had crossed my mind. But right now my concentration was on flying.

Just before reaching the coast, below 50 feet with the airspeed beyond the red line, the P-51s peeled away and left us alone. The lonely feeling returned. A few hundred yards inland, there were about a dozen American tanks parked in a line parallel to the shore. The troops were waving. Not more than half a mile farther inland we passed over a line of moving German tanks that greeted us with machine gun fire. I was unaware that they scored any hits. From here to the drop zone and back to the coast, the sound of enemy fire was heavy.

While flying high, out of range of small arms, you can see the muzzle flash of the antiaircraft fire but can not hear the discharge. When you see the missile explodes, it's not necessarily dangerous. When you hear it – that's bad. When you hear and smell it, watch our. Down here on the deck it seems you can hear every shot, the sound sometimes developing into a roar. I'll never forget the sound of the German machine pistol and bullets hitting the fuselage like hail on a tin roof. The machine pistol fired more rapidly than any automatic weapon in our arsenal, 1500 times a minute. I'll take the high stuff over these low missions anytime.

The Normandy countryside is beautiful, laid out in squares of flat farmland, separated by narrow growths of trees (hedgerows), 20 to 30 feet high. But it didn't look so pretty this morning. There were so many Germans, they had no place to hide. On one field it looked like the Santa Anna parade grounds after dispersal. They were all shooting at one target, me. I remember thinking, "These bastardy are shooting at ME." I never had any feelings of hate for the Germans. Now I had extreme feelings of anger. Scott had opened his side window and was firing his 45 downward. I don't think he was aiming at anything in particular, just shooting. I yelled, "Don't hit the prop."

I was flying so low, the Germans were firing their rifles and machine pistols on a horizontal plane. I tried to hit the enemy with our props, and actually saw some up ahead fall flat on the ground to avoid decapitation.

We had never been taught how to take evasive action from ground fire, and I had never given it much thought. Now, instinct directed the flight. Anything to make them miss. When machine gun tracers were visible, knowing the gunners would lead the longitudinal axis of the airplane, I used almost full rudder and opposite aileron. This caused the airplane to fly nearly sideways. We must have made an awesome sight, so low to the ground, sliding in one direction and then the other. At the far end of one of the fields I was late pulling up and sailed right through the top of a hedgerow. The noise was horrifying, like a giant lawnmower colliding with a freight train. I thought for sure we had 'bought the farm'.

Approaching the drop zone, I closed the throttles, pulled up to 400 feet, and Jim gave the green light to start discharging the cabin bundles. I released the packs underneath. There was no enemy fire now. The crew must have been as terrified as I. They got rid of those supplies in record time. As the last bundle cleared the door, the crew chief came running forward shouting, "All Out! All Out!"

At 400 feet with a fairly slow airspeed, I kicked full left rudder and applied considerable back pressure on the yoke. As the nose came up, the airplane switched ends like a hungry hog. Diving toward the treetops we took hits from what I judged to be a 20- MM antiaircraft gun mounted on the roof of a farmhouse. One hit filled the cockpit with smoke, and I had to open the side window to breathe. Another knocked out the left engine. The prop would not feather, and the vibration was severe. I think one of the blades was shot off. A climb was impossible. We could hardly maintain altitude at minimum speed. There was no evasive action now, I just flew straight and hoped for the best.

As we crossed the coast and enemy fire ceased and I was elated. It looked like the whole US Navy was in front of us. Unable to climb over the ships, we snaked around them. I could see the antiaircraft guns on deck following us all the way. This was cause for worry. During the invasion of Sicily one of our C-47s was shot down by an American destroyer. The crew managed to get into life rafts, but the destroyer continued firing. All crew members were killed except one pilot. Friendly fire can be deadly.

After clearing the fleet, I saw a C-47 ditch with the landing gear down. He went into the up-slope of a swell so deep that only the tail did not go under. Then bobbed up like a cork. I did not see anyone escape.

I had visions of making it to an airport on the English coast, any airport, but not for long. The vibration was getting worse, and now it was almost impossible to read the instruments. We were slowly losing the battle to stay airborne. When it became obvious that this airplane was not going any farther, I ordered Sargent Blake, the radio operator, to send an SOS and lock the key. The choice to land in the raging sea seemed to have been made for me.

We were taught ditching at sea was best accomplished on a heading parallel to the swells. Land in the trough between the swells. I estimated the swells to be 20 feet. The wind was 30 to 40 MPH and gusty, blowing from the same direction as the swells were coming. I elected to land into the wind and the swells. The excitement of the time prohibited any thought of death or any other speculation. When I was a kid, riding with my mother in a Model T Ford, she lost control and sailed off the road into a pine forest. Dodging the trees, just before hitting one, she yelled, "God help us!" And He did. The tail hit the top of a swell and we plowed into the up-slope of the next one. I yelled, "God help us!" And He did.

With our slow forward speed, it wasn't so bad, although without my shoulder harness on, I cracked the windshield with my head as the cockpit buried itself in the water. The impact caused quite a knot on my forehead, which I didn't notice until sometime later. The one time I needed the shoulder harness, I didn't have it connected. I thought the harness to be an impediment to flying.

When the aircraft came to rest, there was no water in the cockpit. A glance back in the cabin revealed a large hole, maybe ten feet long, in the floor. Like a huge can-opener had been at work. I could see control cables and the water below. Scott was pounding on the overhead emergency exit trying to open it. The exit was stuck and required both of us with superhuman strength to pop it outward. It probably had not been opened since the airplane was manufactured. I know the Captain is supposed to be the last to abandon ship, but in this case, I said, "Follow me", as I hoisted myself through the opening to the top of the cockpit.

Scott and the Blake followed, and immediately jumped down to the left wing. My crew chief and the private at the cargo door launched a three-man life raft, and floated it to the two men on the wing. Then they launched another one. I reminded them, "Don't jump in the raft. You will go right through the bottom." Both rafts were moored to the fuselage with a rope.

I was standing on top of the fuselage riding the 20-foot monstrous swells, up and down like a roller coaster. My stomach got that queasy feeling. Funny, it never did that when flying. I watched as Scott tossed his gun and knife into the raging sea. Why he threw away his weapons, puzzles me as much today as it did then. He and the Blake boarded the raft and were immediately blown away from the fuselage, despite my orders to stay together. They tried to paddle, but that was like spitting in the face of a hurricane. It was only a matter of minutes before they were out of sight.

The private was already in the raft at the rear door when I realized that I was not wearing a Mae West. This was a real scare. A Mae West – for the younger generation – is a life jacket. For someone as chicken as me, a poor swimmer, always on the front row at safety lectures, who had extra flak suits on the floor and around my seat; you wouldn't expect this to happen. Before panic completely engulfed me, my crew chief threw one up to me before he jumped from the door and climbed into the raft.

The airplane was floating in an extreme nose down attitude, thus elevating the tail. From where I was standing, it must have been more than 20 feet to the water. According to procedure, you are not supposed to inflate the Mae West until in the water, but I was not about to jump without making sure that this thing was working properly. So I inflated it, and made the highest dive, I've ever made – feet first. Impact with the water, besides causing considerable pain in the crotch, almost stripped away my Mae West. Water was forced up my nose. So ashamed of forgetting my life jacket, I never told anyone till the war was over.

Besides damage to the cabin floor and the left engine, the left wing's trailing edge and flaps were partly shot away, and there were hundreds, if not thousands, of bullet holes all over. I never saw the right side. I don't know how long my aircraft floated, because the only time you could see it was when the ship and raft were on top of a swell at the same time.

The life rafts were small rubber three-man affairs. I climbed aboard with the crew chief and the private, only to find the raft full of bullet holes. There was some air trapped, but not enough to completely support us. Rather than abandon the raft, we sat in it with water up to our waist to be more visible. The wind was really whistling, like riding a sailboat. There was a point of land in the distance, and it appeared that we would be blown ashore. One of my companions asked, "If we are blown ashore, What do we do? Fight?"

"Hell, I don't know."

Laying as low as possible in the crumpled raft, we came so close to the German-held shore, you could see enemy troops running from one emplacement to another. Twice, as we were being blown across the Seine Bay, American fighters buzzed us and rocked their wings. We had been spotted.

We all got a severe case of seasickness and threw up everything eaten the past week. The private complained of back pain. It was later determined that he had a fractured vertebrae. Probably received as he was thrown around the cabin, when I was taking evasive action.

The British Air Sea Rescue Service was largely made up of boats of every diverse description, which were donated and manned by British civilians. Rescue attempts nearer than three miles to enemy-held coast were prohibited, and we were now less than a mile offshore.

After being in the water for four and one half hours, a brave skipper in a forty-foot launch chose to ignore the rules, and hastily took us aboard. Under full power speeding away from the hostile shore, we were given hot coffee and dry clothes (also donated by British civilians). I was given a heavy knitted white wool turtle-neck sweater which reached half way to my knees. I kept the sweater for many years.

The water in the Channel is cold, even in June. My feet were completely numb, and the rest of my body was beginning to feel the effects of the expedition. We would not have survived the night.

I found Lt. Scott huddled below deck. He had been rescued two hours before. I asked where Blake was. "He started vomiting blood and died. I let him go overboard." Jim answered.

I was astounded, because on top of the airplane, Blake had appeared perfectly normal. Although, there was a small laceration on his forehead. I intended to write a letter to his parents, but never did. An omission which, to this day, I sadly regret.

It was after dark when we were put ashore at a British Naval Base in Southern England. We were escorted to a barracks for some rest.

Standing orders after all missions were to be debriefed immediately by an intelligence officer at any US Air Corps Base. I told Scott, "Get the crew back to base anyway you can. I'm going to get debriefed."

It was four A.M. when the US Navy Shore Patrol delivered me to the airport gate of an American fighter group. In a jeep with a MP driver, we searched the base for an intelligence officer. None was found. I asked to see the Commanding Officer.

The CO, a West Point Bird Colonel, housed in a Quonset hut set away from the main complex, was not happy to be awakened at this hour. I gave him a brief rundown of the mission, and he asked, "Anything else?"

"Yeah. A couple of P-51s escorted me across the channel and then abandoned me at the beach. I thought they should have gone all the way."

He laughed, "I don't blame them. They didn't have a prayer in there on the deck."

I started to ask the question, "If those armorplated fast fighters didn't have a chance, what was I doing in there in that slow transport with no self-sealing tanks?" But common sense took over. He was already mad enough.

Dressed in my long white sweater and civilian trousers, with my side arm underneath the sweater, I hitched a ride on a C-47 back to Barkston Heath airdrome. With no identification except my escape kit, no one ever questioned me. I wondered if a German spy could have done the same thing.

As I walked in the door of my miniature Quonset hut at Barkston, my three roommates, Captains Wood, Ward and Minor, jumped up and Wood shouted, "God damn! Clyde, we thought you were dead. We gave all your stuff away!" My corner was totally bare. Even the cot was gone. They let me stew for a few seconds, then gave me a big hug. It was all a joke. They were really glad to see me.

I never considered myself to be a religious person, really never thought much about it. But after the last two days, I had a feeling of nearness to God, that had not been present before. Now with peace of mind and absolute exhaustion, I slept 12 hours. Without my awareness, Clyde's Corner was still developing. You don't have to do everything right to come out alive.

Major Betts, squadron CO, called me to his hut and said, "Clyde, you are the only one that made it to the drop zone and I'm going to recommend you for the DFC (Distinguished Flying Cross). Not for your flying ability, but because you were the only one that had guts enough to go in there." I didn't tell him the only reason I didn't 'go in there' was because it never occurred to me. At that young age, the thought process is not fully developed. Maybe that's why young pilots are preferred in time of war. I thanked him and asked him to recommend the private for a Purple Heart. "I can't do that." He said. "He's a noncombatant and wasn't supposed to be along, but I can recommend you for one. That's quite a bump on your forehead."

"Please don't." Was my reaction. I thought the medal was for more serious injuries.

General Ridgeway pinned the DFC on my Eisenhower Jacket, and they mailed me the Air Medal. Someone sent me a membership in the Goldfish Club, made up of members who had used a rubber dinky for survival.

For some time afterwards, I had a pronounced feeling of serenity and closeness to God. The rest of my life I have wondered if there was anything I could have done differently, that would have prevented the death of one of my crew.

May the good Lord bless you with a good memory and lots of good luck.

Clyde E. Roach

Lightning Source UK Ltd.
Milton Keynes UK
UKOW050109051212

203167UK00001B/273/P